Changing Marketing Strategies in a New Economy

Edited by
Jules Backman
and
John A. Czepiel

Our economy is essentially an economy of
large-scale production. To distribute this
output, marketing plays a crucial role. But
marketing techniques cannot remain static as
the sharply stepped-up pace of competition
and technological change challenges the
marketing man's mettle as never before. How
must both concepts and strategies be changed
to meet the influx of foreign multinational
corporations on our shores? What will be the
social consequences of the shifting pattern of
production, financing, distribution and
consumption?

The sixth Key Issues Lecture Series sponsored
by NYU was devoted to discussing various
aspects of these long-range problems. This
book brings together six widely-respected
authorities. Their overview is supplemented by
a critical analysis by the editors, Jules
Backman and John A. Czepiel. Then Harvard
Professor Theodore Levitt leads off with a
description of how the corporate purpose is
incorporated into the marketing matrix. He
shows why the non free-market economies
have failed to match the extraordinary
efficiency of the Free World.

In the next chapter, Professor Philip Kotler of
Northwestern warns that cases of
overmarketing excesses are beginning to appear.

(Continued on back flap)

(Continued from front flap)

He cites examples of how government action deescalated the competitive spiral, thus breaking the overmarketing stalemate. Former American Marketing Association President Arnold Corbin stresses that the era of "splendid isolation" for planners is over because the team approach better equips firms to cope with scarcities in resources and managerial talent. Keeping all management echelons informed is especially effective in reducing duplication of effort and expense. NYU Professor Gerald J. Glasser's formula for good market research is to balance quality against risk against usefulness against cost. He calls for greater realization that market research data are subject to different kinds of inaccuracies. Crocker National Bank Chairman Thomas R. Wilcox emphasizes that although the market planning process for financial institutions may look the same, the actual strategy is profoundly influenced by other factors. While keeping the "wheels of commerce" turning, banks are also instruments of the monetary system and important conduits of national economic policy. President J. Fred Bucy of Texas Instruments traces how technology has been the prime determinant in electronics. He concludes that equal technology does *not* become quickly available to all participants in science-based businesses. And a balanced interweaving of the creating, making, and marketing functions are necessary for success.

ABOUT THE EDITORS

JULES BACKMAN has been a member of the NYU faculty since 1938. As an economist and nationally-known consultant for government and industry, Dr. Backman has written more than 100 books and pamphlets on numerous business subjects.

JOHN A. CZEPIEL received his PhD. at Northwestern before joining NYU's College of Business and Public Administration faculty in 1972. He has written extensively on marketing concepts and has been active as a consultant for major corporations.

THE KEY ISSUES LECTURE SERIES
is made possible through a grant from
International Telephone and Telegraph Corporation

These lectures were held at the
School of Business and Public Administration
New York University

CHANGING MARKETING STRATEGIES IN A NEW ECONOMY

Edited by

Jules Backman and John Czepiel

With a Foreword by
Harold S. Geneen

Bobbs-Merrill Educational Publishing
Indianapolis

The Bobbs-Merrill Company, Inc.
4300 West 62nd Street
Indianapolis, Indiana 46268

First Edition
First Printing 1977   *036683*

Library of Congress Cataloging in Publication Data
Main entry under title:

Changing marketing strategies in a new economy.

(Key issues lecture series)
    Lectures delivered at the College of Business and Public
Administration, New York University.
    1. Marketing—Addresses, essays, lectures. I. Backman, Jules,
1910-   II. Czepiel, John. III. New York University. College of
Business and Public Administration.
    I.S.B.N. 0-672-97199-2 (Pbk)   658.8   77-11109

    I.S.B.N. 0-672-97198-4   *HF*
                                  5415
                                  .C4826
                                  1977

Contents

Preface

Abraham L. Gitlow

Dean, College of Business and
Public Administration
New York University

The Key Issues Lecture Series at the College of Business and Public Administration, New York University, is now represented by six volumes of these important lectures. This volume, the sixth in the series, collects the papers presented under the general topic *Changing Marketing Strategies In a New Economy*. The topic was selected because of its appropriateness in an economy characterized by large-scale production and a massive outpouring of goods and services, yet characterized also in recent years by major demographic changes and profound shifts in societal values and goals.

The Key Issues Lecture Series has been made possible by a grant from the International Telephone and Telegraph Corporation. Its organizer is Professor Jules Backman, to whom all credit for the series is due. To both ITT and Professor Backman go the College's deep appreciation, for the series has enabled the College to enhance its role in advancing public understanding of many major contemporary issues.

The lecturers whose papers are included in this volume are a distinguished group, and we are completely confident that this volume will receive as excellent a reception as its predecessors have.

My personal appreciation goes also to Professor John Czepiel for his significant contribution; to Catherine Ferfoglia, Professor Backman's secretary and principal aide in preparing the volume for publication; and to my administrative assistants, Susan Greenbaum and Virginia Moress.

Foreword

Harold S. Geneen

Chairman and Chief Executive
International Telephone and Telegraph Corporation

The balance of this century will develop new economic and social relationships within which marketing managers must function. Tomorrow will belong to those managers who can understand *and* adapt to new relationships between owner and user, producer and customer, and the ever-present regulator and regulated.

Several years ago, ITT looked beyond its traditional planning goals to define world markets of the 1980s. Thus, its Project 80 was born: to provide understanding of the new challenges which industry must meet if it is to realize the dual goals of future growth and a more effective rendering of services to people throughout the world.

New skills will be demanded of the marketing professional if he is to be effective in an evolving, dynamic world economy. He must conceptualize the wants of consumers and identify their emerging needs. He must develop ways to meet these new needs as consumer tastes and demands continue to shift, probably more rapidly than ever before. Moreover, he must evaluate the impact of a growing energy shortage, both in terms of the type of goods which will be available and of the erosive effect upon consumer purchasing power.

It is one of the ironies of social change that while new products may contribute to higher standards of living, they also complicate the lives of consumers—and initially require time and effort on the consumer's part to learn about them.

The new breed of marketing professional will require more and different types of training. He must strengthen his command of his most singular skill: the ability to successfully motivate and influence more and more people. Business schools, such as NYU's College of Business and Public Administration, are responding splendidly to these challenges with new and more meaningful marketing programs.

This timely series has offered new approaches to marketing methodology and strategies. From the vantage points of academia and from the business world, six outstanding participants have examined the role marketing must play in tomorrow's world. They have provided incisive insights into the marketing strategies required to achieve successful corporate and social goals. We can all profit from their considerable experience.

Once again, I am grateful to Dr. Jules Backman, who continues to moderate the Key Issues Lecture Series in an exemplary manner. With the assistance of Professor John Czepiel, Dr. Backman also edited the transcript of these proceedings into the coherent distillation presented in this volume.

ONE

Marketing Strategy:

Some Basic Considerations

Jules Backman

Research Professor Emeritus of Economics

and

John A. Czepiel

Associate Professor of Marketing

New York University

Marketing strategy is an integral part of corporate strategy. Corporate strategy is the overall plan for the firm, and marketing strategy is that part of the plan dealing with the utilization of the marketing variables to achieve the plan. As Professor Theodore Levitt notes, "There can be no corporate strategy that is not in some fundamental fashion a marketing strategy, no purpose that does not respond somehow to what people are willing to buy for a price."

CORPORATE STRATEGY

To understand the nature of marketing strategy requires a full understanding of the concept of corporate strategy.[1] Ansoff states that corporate strategy is one which "(1) Provides a broad concept of the firm's business, (2) sets forth specific guidelines by which the firm can conduct its search for markets, and (3) supplements the firm's objectives with decision rules which narrow the firm's selection process to the most attractive opportunities."[2] And Fred Bucy states that the "create, make, and market functions must be tightly interwoven in a system of management, corporate philosophy and the corporate purpose."

Typically, four components of corporate strategy are recognized: (1) market opportunity, (2) corporate competence and resources, (3) the personal values and aspirations of top executives, and (4) acknowledged obligations to segments of society other than the stockholders.[3] These components make clear that corporate strategy is concerned with optimizing the firm's relationships with its environment. As such, it also has an ethical aspect, namely that alternatives must be ordered as much by responsibility as by return on investment. Emphasizing this point, Fred Bucy noted, "The basic purpose of corporations is to exercise wise stewardship in managing a large share of the physical assets of society." Similarly, among financial institutions "the actual strategy developed is profoundly influenced by the fact that banks are instrumentalities of the monetary system and important conduits of economic policy," as Thomas Wilcox stressed.

Given an evaluation of its four components, corporate strategy, according to Philip Kotler, comprises "the broad principles by which the company hopes to secure an advantage over competitors, and attractiveness to buyers, and a full exploitation of company resources."[4]

MARKETING STRATEGY

Marketing strategy includes the firm's plan to follow certain decision paths in each of six areas: product, pricing, distribution, promotion, market selection and approach, and competitive orientation. Marketing strategy recognizes that decisions in these six areas are interrelated and that it is necessary to coordinate individual decisions to achieve synergy so that the combined effect may be greater than the sum of the parts.

Product Strategy. As in the statement of corporate strategy, it is necessary to make certain broad decisions with respect to the firm's product-service mix. This includes an overall determination of a desirable product mix in terms of profit, risk, and growth, standards and criteria for the evaluation of new products as well as old, and broad policies with respect to branding and differentiation.

Pricing Strategy.   The role that pricing is to take in the overall marketing mix must be determined—whether it is to be an actively used tool or one which is deemphasized.[5] In general, the firm will also include some measure of the price level to be pursued, whether premium, or otherwise. These guidelines, of course, will have been achieved through joint analysis with the other factors.

Distribution Strategy.   Channels of distribution represent an integral part of the overall marketing strategy because decisions in this area directly affect all other marketing decisions. This is especially so because they involve long term commitments with other firms and have a long-lasting effect on the firm's future range of alternatives. Professor Theodore Levitt's description of the different distribution strategies pursued by Exxon and Gulf in the 1950s and the results of each illustrate well the long-range consequences of distribution decisions.

Promotional Strategy.   Strategic promotional decisions are of two types. The first concerns the role that promotion is to take in the marketing mix— whether it is to be a major or minor element or whether it is to be left to others. Second is the problem of the promotional mix—the blend of advertising, personal selling, sales promotion, et cetera—that is to be followed by the firm.

Market Selection.   A key to the overall marketing strategy is the selection of markets to be served and the approach to be taken to those markets. Based on the recognition that it is impossible for any one firm to be all things to all people, the firm must determine what segmentation strategy it will pursue and how it will approach different market segments. Professor Philip Kotler calls this process "taking a position in the market."

Competitive Strategy.   Finally, firms must determine what will be their approach to competition and on what basis they will compete. The firm may define its competition on the basis of all products which fill the same need (generic), on the basis of those having a similar form (product form), or on the basis of company or brand (enterprise competition). Marketing strategy involves the predetermination of these factors.

Marketing strategy, from the discussion above, takes the set of goals, objectives, and guidelines from the corporate strategy statement and begins to define the general form, that of marketing activities. It consists of choosing from the complete set of alternatives that smaller set which will best enable the firm to reach its goals in light of the unsatisfied needs of the marketplace and the strategies of its competitors.

STRATEGY FORMULATION

The concept of strategy formulation is a difficult one to capture. There are those, for example, for whom strategy is no problem for they deny that the concept is of any value. There are quite a few firms, some even of good size, which deny that strategic planning or strategy formulation occurs. These firms prefer to feel that top management, merely by sitting down and discussing business, arrives at some consensus which serves to guide the business and charts its future path. Professor Arnold Corbin speaks of such firms as practicing "management by intuition" and of the disadvantages that such procedures entail as businesses and markets both grow and change more rapidly.

Other firms admit that they think about the problems of strategy and may even suggest that one exists. Their strategy, however, is seldom found on paper so that its assumptions and goals may be open to discussion or testing. More likely it is contained in the head of the chief officer.

However, regardless of what a company says, strategy formulation does occur and there are very few firms, whatever their size, which do not have a business strategy or a marketing strategy. While the process and its results may be unconscious, it is a reality.

Ansoff finds that firms fall into one of three classes in their approach to strategy analysis.[6]

1. *Reactors*—firms which wait for problems to occur before they attempt to solve them. Perhaps the unconscious strategizers noted earlier fit into this category.

2. *Planners*—firms which anticipate problems and plan for them.

3. *Entrepreneurs*—firms which anticipate both problems and opportunities. This group incorporates those firms for which the problem of strategic analysis, formulation, and planning is a conscious ongoing effort. Much analysis of the strategy formulation process looks at this last class of firms or assumes that such a firm exists.[7]

Professor Arnold Corbin emphasizes the need for this formal planning effort:

There are four main forces at work in the business world today that make it important to plan marketing strategies systematically, so that full advantage of opportunities may be taken, and thereby long-range targets for growth and profit achieved. These four factors are:

1. The increasing size and complexity of business organizations;
2. The sharply stepped-up pace of competition;
3. The increasingly rapid rate of change in both the technological and marketing environments; and
4. The increasing pressure for new products and markets.

William D. Guth, however, feels that the rigor implied in the conscious approach goes beyond that which may realistically be attained.[8] He sees limitations in the more rigorous approaches because, "in practice, any particular top-level decision maker, even the president, is constrained in his strategic decision making by the fact that others in his organization are likely to have varying conclusions about appropriate strategy commitments."[9]

The relatively unstructured problem of strategy formulation and the differing perceptions that each of the executives concerned brings to the problem makes such variations to be expected. Thus, the refinement of analytical methodology much beyond the level of broad prescription would be fruitless. Guth sees a major problem impeding strategy formulation to be goal consensus, the commitment of the organization to the pursuit of a particular strategy. Professor Gerald Glasser would agree with Guth's conclusions but for other reasons. He sees marketing decision processes as "mostly informal, intuitive, subjective, instinctive and judgmental—whether research is involved or not."

CURRENT DIRECTION IN MARKETING STRATEGY

While many have studied the problem of strategy formulation as noted above, a far smaller number of analysts have studied the content of business and marketing strategies.[10] Three studies, however, are indicative of the essential thrust of current academic and business thinking. They share a common focus on the relationship between market share, marketing variables, and return on investment. Further, Michel Chevalier investigated the relationship between market share and profitability. His findings implied that for certain types of industries—essentially those in which the actions of one firm can affect the market success of the other—companies should seek to dominate those market segments in which they operate. Moreover, his studies suggest that the firm should divest itself of businesses in market segments where their market share is small and where future growth is unlikely. Finally, he suggests that a better strategy is to confine activities to markets in which a firm can be dominant, even if this means operating in a smaller market.[11]

The Boston Consulting Group has pursued and refined the concept of the experience curve to the point where this essentially production phenomenon has strong implications for marketing strategy.[12] They suggest that firms should try to gain a high share of a market very early in the product life cycle. This conclusion is based on the experience curve which indicates that total per unit costs decrease in direct relationship to the cumulative experience and market share. Thus the company with the largest share should be able to maintain the lowest cost. This principle is well demonstrated by Fred Bucy in Fig. 7.2, p. 136, where only the firm with the largest cumulative volume is able to operate at an acceptable profit level. The Boston Consulting Group's research implies that new products must be sold at prices below total costs until volume builds up and that eventually, prices must go down as fast as costs, if there is any competition at all in the industry. Lastly, they posit that market shares will be unstable until one producer clearly dominates the market and its prices are low enough to inhibit growth in the relative market share of any significant competitor or until market growth stops. Of course this does not mean that market shares will be rigid and inflexible once this point is reached, but rather that the great and frequent shifts in leadership, such as those which occur in the rapid growth stage of the life cycle, are less likely to be observed.

The studies of Schoeffler et al. have yielded findings which are somewhat similar.[13] Based on actual data for some sixty firms in over 800 individual businesses, they find that a high return on investment (ROI) is related to a strong market position. This is accentuated where the purchase frequency is low, the production cycle long, and the manufacturing intensity is low. Given a strong market position, the ROI can be further enhanced by increasing product differentiation. These studies show that in mature markets high relative prices are only slightly more profitable than average prices and that low prices are significantly less profitable than either high or medium product prices.

The thrust in strategic marketing thinking described above indicates the kinds of developments which are likely to emerge in the future. Corporate management appears ready to implement those strategies which are based on sound theoretical and empirical work and, indeed, it is actively involved in the development of research designed to uncover such strategies.

FORCES AFFECTING MARKET STRATEGIES

Marketing strategy cannot remain static in a dynamic economy. As Professor Theodore Levitt noted, quoting popular philosophy: "Nothing is so constant as change." Some of the forces which will contribute to our changing economy and influence marketing strategies in the years ahead include: a slower rate of population growth, a probable slower growth in the national economy than in the past, changes in the nature of our society, persistent price inflation, new attitudes toward the social responsibility of business, a continuing information explosion, and an expanding role for government. Marketing strategies will have to cope with and adapt to these and other forces hidden by the veil of the future. In the words of Professor Theodore Levitt, "The market calls the tune, and the players better play it right."

Slower Rate of Population Growth

The post-World War II baby boom has provided an enlarged market for a changing mix of products during the past three decades. As the larger number of babies moved down the stream of life, opportunities were provided for producers of the many goods and services required to meet their needs. In the beginning of the boom, the greatest benefits went to those serving the needs of the new babies and young children. Later, the flood tide required an expansion of elementary school facilities, and then, in time, high schools and colleges had to expand their plants and faculties. Along the way, the teenage market burgeoned. They are now reaching marriageable age with the consequent opportunities for those supplying the needs for new and growing families.

However, this population wave has crested. The number of new births has declined as the birth rate has fallen markedly from 25.3 per 1000 in 1957 to 14.8 in 1975. In 1975, the total number of births was 3,149,000 as compared with more than 4.2 million per year from 1957 to 1961.[14]

As a result, the U.S. Bureau of the Census is projecting a slower rate of population growth for the next quarter of a century. As compared with total population of 214 million, the total is projected at 262.5 million for the year 2000. The annual rate of increase will be only 0.8% as compared with 1.4% in the preceding quarter of a century. In actual numbers the projected increase is 48.5 million as compared with 63 million in the preceding twenty-five years.[15]

In connection with these projections it is well to keep in mind that in the past they often have been far off the mark. For example, in the 1930s it was anticipated that total population would level off in several decades while in the mid-1960s some optimistic projections had the population at about 318 million in 2000.[16] Nevertheless, there appear to be solid grounds for anticipating a continuation of the slowdown in population growth. The widespread use of the pill and other birth control devices, shifting attitudes toward family life as reflected in the sharply rising divorce rates, later marriages, and the changing role of women all point to a continuation of lower birth rates than in the earlier post-World War II years. Thus, the U.S. Department of Labor has forecast that 51.4% of women 16 years of age and over will be in the civilian labor force in 1990 in contrast to 43.0% in 1970.[17] Since the percentage had already reached 48.1% in November, 1976,[18] the 1990 projected figure may turn out to be too low.

A steadily increasing proportion of the population consists of senior citizens. The proportion has increased from 4.1% in 1900 and from 8.1% in 1950 to 10.5% in 1975 and is projected at 12% for the year 2000.[19]

The products and services consumed by senior citizens are significantly different from those demanded by younger members of the population. The size of their families is smaller, their average incomes lower; there is less replacement of home furnishings and clothing; they have a different mix of expenditures with a greater percentage spent on food and health care, et cetera.[20] Moreover, these senior citizens will have to be supported by those who are working. As the proportion of retirees increases, the social security tax burden on workers will continue to rise, as has been the case in recent years. One result is a reduction in the proportion of wages which will represent current spendable income for workers. For example, the social security rate was originally 1% on the first $3,000 of wages and by 1977 it was 5.85% on the first $16,500.

Thus, although the total population will continue to increase, a larger part of the total will be accounted for by this older group which does not have the same affluence nor provide the same market for optional spending as the younger groups. These population trends, therefore, will require a significant shift in marketing strategies in the closing years of the twentieth century. Further, within age groups, different marketing strategies will have to be developed. The growing segmentation of the market will be a prime consideration for marketers in the years ahead.

Future Growth of American Economy

The American economy has expanded at an annual rate of 3.5% to 4.0% in the past. As a result, total gross national product in real terms (constant prices) has doubled about every 20 years. There is no assurance that these growth rates will continue in the future. Some groups have been warning that a shortage of raw materials will act as a barrier to maintaining past growth rates. Higher cost energy and conservation measures will act to slow down growth rates. In the United States, the slower projected rate of population growth could shave the annual growth rate by at least 0.5 percentage point.

In addition, emphasis upon environmental factors has been diverting our limited capital resources from investment in plant expansion to cleaning up pollution. The continuing shift to a service economy will slow up the increase in productivity gains which have been largest in manufacturing and other sectors where the application of large-scale capital investments has added significantly to increases in output per man-hour (OPM).[21]

Despite these constraining forces, the underlying forces contributing to economic growth should continue to operate. Although *the rate of increase in population* will tend to be slower, there will still be an increase in output because more persons will have to be fed, clothed, housed, entertained, et cetera. Continuing large expenditures for research and development portends further technological advances with accompanying increases in OPM.

Again, although the rate of increase probably will be somewhat lower than in the past, there will still be an increase. However, some forecasters assume that the current patterns of resource use will continue and that growth will be restricted by an inadequate supply of raw materials. In the past, such doomsday projections consistently have underestimated the effects of technological improvement adaptation. Society always has found ways to economize on the use of scarce resources and will do so again.

A few figures suggest the range of potential increases in real gross natural product (GNP). In 1975, real GNP was $1,186 billion in 1972 dollars. If the increase in the next quarter of a century were at the past rates of 3.5% to 4.0%, total GNP in 2000 would be $2,803 to $3,166 billion in 1972 dollars. A growth rate of 3% would result in a total of $2,483 billion in 2000 or more than double the 1975 total. A 2.5% growth rate would yield $2,200 billion or an increase of 85%. Thus, even the lowest projected growth rates indicate a significant expansion in the total size of the market.

Another aspect of our economy which can have a profound effect on marketing opportunities is the increasing importance of services as is shown in Table 1.1.

Table 1.1

GROWTH OF SELECTED SERVICE AREAS, 1947-75

	Percentage of Gross National Product				
	1947	1950	1960	1970	1975
State & local government	5.4	6.8	9.2	12.5	14.1
Federal government	5.4	6.5	10.6	9.9	8.2
All services	21.5	21.9	25.6	26.8	28.5
Medical care	3.0	3.1	3.8	4.8	4.9
Housing	6.8	7.5	9.2	9.3	9.9
Auto repair, rentals etc.	0.9	0.9	1.0	0.9	1.3
Private education & research	0.5	0.6	0.7	1.1	1.0
Personal business	2.3	2.4	3.0	3.6	3.3

Source: U.S. Department of Commerce, Bureau of Economic Analysis

Further increases in the relative importance of services are probable in the balance of this century. The relative role of marketing in these service areas generally has been small. However, as one observer has indicated, "New industries and products have already been developed to meet the needs of people who are looking for additional things and new ways to occupy their leisure time."[22]

Lower growth rates will provide a major challenge to marketers. Significant changes in marketing strategy and practice will be necessary. For example, the shift in electric utility advertising from emphasis upon unlimited expansion of consumption to how to limit consumption and how to time its use more effectively provides a dramatic case in point. In some instances, a firm's future market share growth probably will depend on shifts of volume from other firms, rather than upon expansion of the total market.

Nevertheless, even the more modest annual rate of increase—which is probable—would mean an expansion of marketing opportunities for the remainder of this century. However, against the background of smaller rates of increase for the economy, competition will be more intense and a greater premium will be placed upon imaginative programs. Past practices will have to be carefully reviewed and new priorities will be required if the results of marketing programs are to be maximized. Professor Arnold Corbin has stated concisely the marketer's problem: " . . . how to survive and hopefully grow, in a *low-growth* or, possibly, a *no-growth* economy."[23]

Changing Nature of Society

Since the end of World War II, significant changes have taken place in the nature of our society. These have included: (1) an increase in permissiveness; (2) significant changes in the role of the family with greater emphasis upon the nuclear family rather than the extended family; (3) earlier retirement from the work force; (4) older people living by themselves to an increasing extent with the resulting development of retirement communities; (5) health care costs increasingly handled through government as a result of Medicare and Medicaid; (6) increasing acceptance of divorce; (7) court rulings, legislation, and new social awareness which have contributed to a mass attack on discrimination of all types—color, sex, age, economic conditions, education; (8) and women's liberation combined with the above developments which has resulted in an expanded participation in the labor force by women.

Additional significant developments have included: (9) the increasing concern with the quality of life; (10) the efforts to reduce pollution of all kinds—air, water, noise; (11) the decay of the central city; (12) changing life styles as a larger proportion of the population has moved to suburbia, exurbia, and to the sunbelt; and (13) the greater proportion of our youths going to college and into graduate work.

The changing role of women and of minority groups is painted in broad strokes below. An increasing proportion of the labor force consists of women—today more than four out of every ten workers. This compares with three out of ten in 1950 and two out of ten at the beginning of this century. The upward trend in labor force participation has been due almost solely to the increased participation rate of married women—from 23.8% in 1950 to 44.4% in 1975.[24]

The increase in job opportunities for women has been affected by the growth of the service sector noted earlier. Women traditionally have had more job opportunities in this area since it offers more white collar employment and affords more opportunities for part-time work, a vital factor for those with young children. The increase in their formal education combined with the equal pay for equal work movement has helped to raise the salaries women can command.

The impact of these developments has been profound and will likely continue in the same direction in the future. New social and economic attitudes as to the role of women in our society have had and will continue to have substantial influence on marketing. Thus, from an era early in this century that emphasized canning and baking at home we are now in a time period that emphasizes prepackaged and frozen foods. Time and labor-saving appliances in the home have assumed an ever-increasing role.

Similarly, the role of minorities is improving. Though much remains to be done to wipe out discrimination, progress has been made in the past two decades. There has been some narrowing of the income gap; employment opportunities have increased in many industries; educational opportunities have improved; and there has been increased availability of training. Thus, the median black income in relation to that for whites increased from around 50% in the late fifties to slightly more than 60% in 1970.[25] The civil rights activities of the 1950s and 1960s have opened up many levels of jobs not previously available to blacks, a trend which should accelerate as they receive more training in the years ahead. One result will be a further narrowing of the income gap.

A decade ago the Council of Economic Advisers indicated the benefits to society from income equality by noting: "If both unemployment rates and productivity levels [of blacks and whites] were equalized, the total output of the economy would rise by about $27 billion—4% of GNP. This is a measure of the annual economic loss as a result of discrimination."[26] It also is one measure of the gains that are possible in our national economy as economic discrimination is reduced.

These changes indicate the creation of marketing opportunities for some firms as well as the necessity of shifting existing strategies for others. The generally improving economic condition of blacks and other minorities has created markets where they previously did not exist. The past has seen strong growth among those firms which have sought to serve this market and continuance of this trend appears likely. The shifts in the status of women in society are, however, more difficult to predict and to relate to marketing strategy. One might see, for example, a lessening in the concern of women with household cleaning tasks and, hence, in the demand for the products used in these tasks. A lowered level of concern as the homemaker's focus of attention shifts beyond the household may require changes in product characteristics and even in the packaging and distribution of the product as store visits are reduced and efficiency becomes more important. Paralleling this development is the likelihood of a change in the orientation of business toward its role in society. According to Professor Philip Kotler, some companies "are trying to define their business mission in the broadest possible human terms. . . . Hand-in-hand with creating a human-centered mission will go changes in marketing practices that will reflect a more humanistic approach to customers and their needs."

Price Inflation

Consumer buying patterns have been significantly influenced by the ongoing price inflation of the past decade. Since 1965, consumer prices have increased steadily, culminating in the double digit rate of price inflation in 1974. The rate of inflation abated considerably to about 6% in 1976.

Between 1965 and 1976, the consumer price index rose by 80.4%. The overall rate of inflation reflects widely varying rates of increases in different sectors of the economy. Thus, retail food prices increased 91.5% and medical care 106.4%, while the prices of apparel rose 57.5% and those of transportation 72.6%.

Because of these diverse rates of increase in prices, the proportion of the consumer dollar spent on food increased from 22.4% to 23.7%, while that for apparel declined from 10.6% to 9.2% and for transportation from 13.9% to 13.5%.

The overall rate of price inflation was affected by special developments such as the Arab oil boycott in 1973 and Russian wheat purchases. However, the basic forces creating price inflation are found in the large deficits in the federal budget, large increases in money supply, and the enormous increases in labor costs.

With the exception of the fiscal year 1969, the federal government has operated in the red in each year since 1965; the deficit was enormous in 1975 and 1976. The great increase in expectations of many groups—which politicians have encouraged and supported—has contributed significantly to this record since the large budgetary deficits reflect mainly the enormous growth in social welfare programs. There is no evidence that these expenditures are being brought under control so that this fundamental source of inflation is still present and probably will be important in the years ahead.

During the 1965-75 period, monetary policy also contributed to the overall price inflation by facilitating increases in money supply in excess of the increases in real gross national product (GNP). Thus, from 1965 to 1975, currency-plus-demand deposits (M-1) rose by 73.0% and the total, including time deposits at commercial banks other than large certificates of deposit (M-2), increased by 121.6% in contrast to the increase of only 28.1% in real GNP.

The great increase in expectations combined with the developing price inflation has played a significant role in the enormous rise in wages and in other labor costs, far in excess of the gains in output per man-hour. The result has been a large increase in unit labor costs as shown in Table 1.2.

Table 1.2

PERCENT INCREASES IN UNIT LABOR COSTS, 1965-75

	Total Private Economy	Private NonFarm Economy
Compensation per hour	104.4%	100.3%
Output per man-hour	18.7	15.8
Unit labor costs	72.3	73.0

This sharp rise in labor costs has contributed to the pressure for higher prices. In effect, it was underwritten by the inflationary fiscal and monetary policies noted above. To the extent that worker's expectations continue to exceed realizable gains in output, there will be continuing pressure for higher prices from this source.

The ongoing price inflation also has contributed to the anticipation that there is a built-in inflation in the economy. This inflationary bias affects companies' decisions in planning new investment and inventory policy and the significance of reported profits. It also influences consumers' spending and saving patterns.[27]

However, the rate of price inflation and its relative impact on different sectors of the economy is not predictable. The result will be continuing uncertainty in this area and a need to keep marketing strategies highly flexible to be able to adjust to ever-changing situations.

Information Revolution

Over the past third of a century, there has been a tremendous expansion in the scope of scientific inquiry as well as a substantial acceleration in the speed with which new knowledge has been put to use. Our dynamic economy requires increasingly more sophisticated information while revolutionary developments in computer technology are making the required information available.[28] The end of these improvements is not yet in sight nor have all of the potential uses of these data for marketing decisions been fully developed.

John Diebold, a pioneer in information technology, has pointed out the speed with which the computer now performs:

> In the mere half second that it takes for spilled coffee to drip from table to floor, today's large computer can:
> Debit 2000 checks to 300 different bank accounts, and examine electrocardiograms of 100 patients, and score 150,000 answers on 3000 exams concurrently evaluating the effectiveness of the questions, and figure the payroll for a company with 1000 employees.[29]

Until the last decade, the impact of the computer on marketing operations was very modest. In more recent years, however, it has been used to manage retail inventories, to identify the best prospects for selected merchandise, to improve the accuracy in the selection of media by advertising agencies, and to develop marketing strategies.

New marketing techniques based on the computer are constantly being improved. Dean Edward M. Mazze has described one development which may have great potential and which would influence retailing significantly:

> . . .   Many convenience goods are amenable to highly centralized, mechanized, and computerized distribution techniques. Such items are marketed through a few large distribution centers in each major market area. Retail transactions are completed by electronic telecommunication push button devices installed in the home. Shopping is done in the home by using a closed circuit television screen mounted on the wall. A direct shop console is connected to the distribution center. Shopping is done by pressing product code buttons to get information on the merchandise. The order is placed by punching buttons to register the items and quantities wanted, tallies are taken and totaled, and the shopping is done in less than ten minutes. The computer confirms the order, clears payment with the bank, and gets the order filled and on its way. At the distribution center, everything is handled by a computer which receives, interprets, and processes the order and schedules it for distribution. Parts of this system are already in operation.[30]

Marketing research has become an increasingly sophisticated tool as more data have become available and as marketing men have learned to harness the capability of the computer. New developments in these areas will affect significantly the development of marketing strategies in the years ahead.

Expanding Role of Government

Increasingly, government regulations have restricted the options available to the marketing strategist. The role that marketing and the marketplace are to play has received considerable attention and, as a result, definite expectations, prescriptions, and sanctions have evolved. Marketing's role in society and, therefore, the strategies it may employ are being subjected to greater societal control and scrutiny. Since the past is a prologue to the future the developments in this area must be kept in mind.[31] Thomas Wilcox's comments serve to highlight the extent of the governmental role in the determination of strategy. "Market planning in a financial institution perforce continually bumps against regulatory boundaries. Interest rate ceilings affect pricing strategy. Restrictions on branching affect distribution strategy. Reserve requirements affect lending strategy."

Market Control. Since the early 1900s—the days of the trust busters—it has been an article of faith that monopoly power is contrary to the economic well-being of the country. But in general, while avoidance of the reality or appearance of monopoly power has been a major element of most marketing strategies, in actuality a cornerstone of marketing strategy has been to gain market dominance or leadership for a product or service.

Recent court rulings, however, have raised some real questions about the long-run acceptability of this strategy. Perhaps the clearest illustration of this trend is the legal action initiated against the five major breakfast cereal manufacturers, seeking to break up the industry, for allegedly participating in a "shared monopoly.[32]" This novel legal approach clearly has future implications for many other industries and strategies if found to be legally enforceable.

Similarly, corrective action has been proposed against Borden in connection with its Realemon brand of concentrated lemon juice.[33] In the Realemon case, the hearing examiner found that, while the means by which the brand's market share was achieved were in themselves not illegal, the tactics it used to maintain market dominance were. The examiner recommended a drastic course of action to remedy the situation—that Borden be required to license the brand name Realemon to other firms.

IBM, which was cited for announcing "new" products far in advance of their actual introduction and delivery, provides another illustration.[34] It was charged that this action was taken solely for the purpose of delaying potential customers from purchasing competitive equipment. This trend to restrict market dominance also is found in actions taken or contemplated against legal monopolies. The telephone industry, beginning with the Carterphone case has been one target.[35] The actions in the cases cited above, if extended to other companies and products—which seems probable, will have a significant impact on marketing strategy in the years ahead.[36]

Channel and distribution strategy. A cornerstone of many marketing strategies has been the granting of exclusive distribution rights in defined geographical territories. Recent rulings have questioned the legality of this strategy.[37] Proposed restrictions have extended beyond the question of legality. Minority and ghetto groups have challenged store location policies which avoided sites in lower income areas.[38] These groups have argued that they have a right to the convenience, low prices, and services that are available in well-known supermarket chains and that it was the chains' responsibility to locate stores in their neighborhoods. At the same time, developers of shopping centers and malls have been required to file environmental impact statements, slowing their development in some markets. As concern over social responsibility expands, these pressures will continue in the future and influence the practices followed by marketers.

Promotional strategy. As one of the most visible tools of marketing strategy, promotional efforts have been the focus of many actions which have served to restrict the ways in which they may be used. The federal government has taken a much larger role in recent years as watchdog and in mandating what advertising may and should contain. Entire industries have been required to document their advertising claims that product X does shave 50% closer or that product Y does contain 50% fewer calories.[39] Other industries have been required to inform consumers about certain features of their products.[40] The automotive industry must include mileage ratings as determined by the Environmental Protection Agency, cigarettes must display statements about their probable link to cancer, energy consumption by appliances is now required on labels, and nutrient labeling and advertising has been the subject of some criticism.

The Federal Trade Commission has brought actions in connection with a number of products (e.g., foods, toys, drugs, and gasoline) to change their advertising claims and in some instances has required that future advertising call attention to misleading claims in the past.

In December 1975, the FTC issued a corrective advertising order against Listerine providing the company was to include in its future advertising the following corrective message: "Contrary to prior advertising, Listerine will not prevent colds or sore throats or lessen their severity." For this purpose, Warner-Lambert is to spend an amount equal to its average budget for Listerine for the ten years from 1962 to 1972. Warner-Lambert appealed this cease and desist order and the FTC was upheld by the U.S. Court of Appeals.[41]

Similarly, an action was brought by the Federal Trade Commission accusing Firestone Tire and Rubber of violating an order forbidding misrepresentation as to safety claims. Firestone agreed to spend at least $750,000 for commercials and advertisements on tire safety. The public, through this advertising, is to be informed that no tires are safe under all conditions of use and that in order to have adequate tire safety the consumer must take necessary measures for proper maintenance.[42]

Government actions have been accompanied by those of private parties. Women's groups have taken advertisers to task for their depiction of women.[43] Examples include the depiction of women primarily in domestic roles, thereby reinforcing traditional stereotyping, and the use of women in sexually demeaning situations—for example, the National Airlines "Fly Me" campaign. [44]

Equally vociferous have been the protests of citizens and public interest groups concerning advertising to children. As a result, both the amount of advertising allowed on children's programs as well as its content have been curtailed. No longer may ads for toys be built around special photographic effects or fantasizing.[45] Instead, they must show the toy in actual use for a specified amount of time in each commercial. A consumer group, on another front, has taken colleges and universities to task because of the content of their promotional efforts. They have called for more truth, with colleges being required to advise prospective students of the numbers of its graduates entering professional and graduate schools and the starting salaries its graduates command in the marketplace.

Societal scrutiny and control with its impact on marketing strategy is perhaps most advanced in the area of promotion. Not only has the range of alternatives been restricted, but marketers must also perform certain tasks in their promotional programming. Professor Philip Kotler sees a move in this area to control not only the quantity of advertising but the quality as well. It is no longer only "here is what you can't do," but also "here is what you have to do if you wish to advertise."[46]

Product Strategy. Similar restrictions, proscriptions, and prescriptions also have been developing in the product sector. Of course, the question of product safety has been of concern for years, dating back to the original Food, Drug and Cosmetics Act of 1906. Societal control of product form has also been on the rise recently, however, as indicated by legislative trends and proposals. In late 1975, for example, the Congress had before it a number of bills relating to product regulation including the Open Dating Perishable Food Act which would have required packaged perishables and semiperishable foods to show clearly the date beyond which they must not be sold.[47] This practice is now in effect for milk and dairy products, bread, and other products.

One of the most interesting bills proposed concerned product testing. This bill would have enabled the Federal Trade Commission (or some other agency) to establish product testing standards for major household appliances and other complicated consumer products. Further, it would be required that these test results be made public, at least at the point of sale, by manufacturers. Proponents of such legislation believed that a) a consumer who is able to make informed comparisons will force the marketplace to become more competitive, and b) that it would put small manufacturers in a better position to compete on the basis of product quality. Such legislation clearly follows in the footsteps of such earlier, enacted legislation as the Consumer Product Safety Act, which in its short existence has issued product standards relating to safety in many areas ranging from children's toys to matches.

Such regulations have both positive and negative aspects and, at times, it is difficult to determine where the correct balance lies. As Thomas Wilcox noted, "The problem. . . . is not the fact of government regulation; it is the character and quality of it." Clearly, today's marketing strategist must be a broken field runner, traversing the field between what his organization can do and is interested in doing, that which the consumer needs and wants, and that which society collectively allows and requires him to do.

NOTES

1. Theodore Levitt, "Marketing Myopia," *Harvard Business Review* (September-October 1975): pp. 26-44, 172-81.
2. H. Igor Ansoff, *Corporate Strategy* (New York: McGraw-Hill, 1965), p. 104.
3. C. Roland Christensen, Kenneth R. Andrews, and Joseph L. Bower, *Business Policy,* Third Edition (Homewood, Ill.: Richard D. Irwin, 1973), p. 110.
4. Philip Kotler, *Marketing Management,* Second Edition (Englewood Cliffs, N.J.: Prentice-Hall, 1972), p. 370.
5. Jules Backman, *Pricing: Policies and Practices* (New York: The Conference Board, 1961).
6. Ansoff, *Corporate Strategy,* p. 208.
7. See, for example, Harold W. Henry, *Long Range Planning Practice in 45 Industrial Companies* (Englewood Cliffs, N.J.: Prentice Hall, 1967); George A. Steiner, *Pitfalls in Comprehensive Long Range Planning* (Oxford, Ohio: Planning Executives Institute, 1972); and Richard F. Vancil and Peter Lorange, "Strategic Planning in Diversified Companies," *Harvard Business Review* (January-February 1975): pp. 81-90.
8. William D. Guth, "Toward A Social System Theory of Corporate Strategy," *The Journal of Business* (July 1976): pp. 374-88.
9. *Ibid.,* p. 375.
10. For a complete review of these studies, see Charles W. Hofer, "Towards a Contingency Theory of Business Strategy," *Academy of Management Journal,* (December 1975): pp. 784-810.
11. Michel Chevalier, "The Strategy Spectre Behind Your Market Share," *European Business* (1972): pp. 63-72.
12. The Boston Consulting Group, Inc., *Perspectives on Experience* (Boston: The Boston Consulting Group, 1970).
13. Sidney Schoeffler, "Profit Impact of Marketing Strategy," *Marketing Science Institute Working Paper,* (November 1972); Sidney Schoeffler, Robert D. Buzzell, and Donald F. Heany, "The Impact of Strategic Planning on Profit Performance," *Harvard Business Review,* (March-April 1974): pp. 137-45; "Schoeffler-Cope Team Tells How PIMS Academic-Business Search for Basic Principles Can Get Line Managers into Strategic Planning," *Marketing News,* 16 July 1976, pp. 6-7; Robert D. Buzzell, Bradley T. Gale, and Ralph G. M. Sutton, "Market Share—A Key to Profitability", *Harvard Business Review* (January-February 1975): pp. 97-106.
14. *Statistical Abstract of the United States, 1963* (Washington: U.S. Department of Commerce, Bureau of the Census, 1963), p. 52; *Monthly Vital Statistics Report, Pro-*

visional Statistics, Annual Summary for the United States, 1975 (Washington: U.S. Department of Health, Education, and Welfare, Public Welfare Service, Health Resources Administration, National Center for Health Statistics, 1976), p. 1.

15. The Bureau of the Census makes three estimates for 2000, namely, 278.0 million, 262.5 million, and 245.1 million. The projection of 262.5 million assumes an average of 2.1 births per woman as compared with 3.2 births in the early 1950s. The figures in the text would be a little different if the high or low projection were used. From *Current Population Reports,* Series P-25, 10, No. 541 (Washington: U.S. Department of Commerce, Bureau of the Census, February 1975), pp. 1, 2. Earlier estimates by the Census Bureau were considerably higher; the range was between 271 and 322 million in *Statistical Abstract of the United States, 1972* (Washington: U.S. Department of Commerce, Bureau of the Census, 1972), p. 7.

16. See, for example, Herman Kahn and Anthony J. Wisner, *The Year 2000* (New York: Macmillan,1967), p. 168.

17. *The U.S. Labor Force in 1990: New Projections* (Washington: U.S. Department of Labor, Bureau of Labor Statistics, September 1976), p. 4.

18. *Employment and Earnings* (Washington, D.C.: U.S. Department of Labor, U.S. Bureau of Labor Statistics, December 1976), p. 23.

19. Derived from *Economic Report of the President,* January 1976 (Washington: 1976), p. 195; *Statistical Abstract of the United States, 1975* (Washington: U.S. Department of Commerce, Bureau of the Census, 1975), p. 6; and *Social and Economic Characteristics of the Older Population, 1974,* Series p-23, No. 57 (Washington: U.S. Department of Commerce, Bureau of the Census, 1975), p. 3.

20. For detailed descriptions of the composition of budgets of retired people and active working people see *City Worker Family Budget,* Bulletin 1575-1, and *Retired Couple's Budget,* Bulletin 1570-4 (Washington: U.S. Department of Labor, Bureau of Labor Statistics, 1966), various pages.

21. See Jules Backman, ed., "Past Growth and Future Prospects" in *Business and the American Economy, 1776-2001,* (New York: New York University Press, 1976), pp. 13-21.

22. Edward M. Mazze, "Marketing in Turbulent Times: The Challenges and the Opportunities" in *1975 Combined Proceedings of American Marketing Association,* p. xxvi.

23. Arnold Corbin, "Changing Patterns in the Kaleidoscope of Marketing" in *1975 Combined Proceedings of AMA,* p. xix.

24. *A Statistical Portrait of Women in the U.S.,* Current Population Reports, Special Studies, Series P23, No. 58 (Washington, D.C.: U.S. Department of Commerce, Bureau of the Census, April 1976, p. 71 and *Marital and Family Characteristics of the Labor Force, March 1975,* Special Labor Force Report 183 (Washington, D.C.: U.S. Department of Labor, Bureau of Labor Statistics, 1976).

25. *Economic Report of the President,* January 1966 (Washington: Council of Economic Advisers, 1966), pp. 108-9 and *New York Times,* 24 July 1974.

26. *Economic Report of the President,* January 1966, p. 110.

27. For some of the adjustments made during the 1975 recession, see "Shifts in Supermarket Buying Patterns," *The Nielsen Researcher* 2 (1975): pp. 2-12.

28. Donald H. Sanders, *Computers and Management in a Changing Society,* Second Edition, (New York: McGraw Hill, 1974), p. 50, and Thomas R. Prince, *Information Systems for Management Planning and Control,* Third Edition (Homewood, Ill.: Richard Irwin, 1975), p. 8.

29. John Diebold, "The Evolving Role of Business Information," in *Business and the American Economy, 1776-2001,* p. 178.

30. Mazze, *1975 Combined Proceedings of AMA,* p. xxvii.

31. For a review of recent developments, see "The Escalating Struggle Between the FTC and Business," *Business Week,* 13 December 1976, pp. 52-59.

32. R. L. Gordon, "Cereal Case Begins as FTC Seeks End to Shared Monopoly," *Advertising Age,* 3 May 1976, p. 1.

33. "An FTC Challenge to Trademark Rights," *Business Week,* 20 September 1976, p. 37.

34. "IBM the Printout Reads 'More Trouble'," *Business Week,* 22 December 1973, p. 33.

35. "The Justice Department Aims at AT&T Again," *Business Week,* 8 December 1973, p. 41.

36. "Deregulation Scares an Industry," *Business Week,* 25 October 1976, p. 37.

37. See for example, C. Burke Tower, "High Court to Rule on Interrelated Competition in Sylvania Case," *Marketing News,* 31 December 1976, p. 7.

38. Donald F. Sexton, Jr., *Groceries in the Ghetto* (Lexington, Mass.: D. C. Heath, 1973).

39. "Back on the Warpath Against Deceptive Ads," *Business Week,* 19 April 1976, p. 148.

40. "Legal Developments in Marketing," *Journal of Marketing* (April 1976), pp. 97-98.

41. See *Journal of Marketing* (July 1976), pp. 101-2; see also "Back on the Warpath against Deceptive Ads," *Business Week,* 19 April 1976, pp. 148-49 and *Wall Street Journal,* 3 August 1977, p. 7.

42. *Trade Cases,* 1976-1, (Chicago, Ill.: Commerce Clearing House, 1976), pp. 68, 134-47.

43. See, for example, A. Belkaoui and J. M. Belkaoui, "Comparative Analysis of the Role Portrayed by Women in Print Advertisements: 1958, 1970, 1972," *Journal of Marketing Research* (May 1976): pp. 168-72; and Lawrence H. Wortzel and John

M. Frisbee, "Women's Role Portrayal Preference in Advertisements: An Empirical Study," *Journal of Marketing* (October 1974): pp. 41-46.

44. "National Airlines Planes and its Already-Controversial New Advertising Campaign Both Set To Take Air November 1," *Wall Street Journal,* 31 October 1975, p. 2.

45. "Legal Developments in Marketing," *Journal of Marketing* (October 1976), p. 119.

46. See, for example, "FTC Readies Language Experts to Argue for Strict Drug Rules," *Advertising Age,* 14 February 1977, p. 2 and "The FTC's Ad Rules Anger Industry," *Business Week,* 1 November 1976, p. 30.

47. John A. Czepiel, *Consumerism, Consumers and the Corporation* (New York: Neil Miles, Ltd., 1975).

TWO

Marketing and the Corporate Purpose

Theodore Levitt

Professor of Business Administration

Graduate School of Business Administration

Harvard University

Nothing in business is so remarkable as the conflicting variety of success formulas offered by its numerous practitioners and professors. And if, in the case of practitioners, they're not exactly "formulas," they're explanations of "how we did it," implying with firm control over any fleeting tendencies towards modesty, that "that's how *you* ought to do it." Practitioners, spurred on by both pride and money, turn themselves thereby into prescriptive philosophers, filled mostly with hot air.

Professors, on the other hand, know better than to deal merely in explanations. We traffic, instead, in higher goods, like *analysis, concepts,* and *theories.* In short, *truth.* Filled thus with self-importance, we turn ourselves thereby hopefully into wanted advisors, consultants filled mostly with woolly congestion.

I do not wish with these words to disparage either—but, instead, to suggest that these two quite legitimately different and respectable professions usually diminish rather than enhance their reputations when intruding too much or with too little thought on each other's turfs.

How often have we heard executives of venerable age and high repute, and entrepreneurs flushed with recent wealth pronounce with lofty certainty and imperial rectitude exactly what produces business success—telling, however, in cleaned-up retrospection, only the story of how they themselves happen to have done it? Listen to ten, and you'll generally get ten different pieces of advice.

Listen to ten professors, and you'll generally get advice by some multiple greater than ten. The difference is not that professors believe more firmly in abundance. Rather, besides teaching, professors are also paid to think. Hence, lacking direct experience, they are likely to think up several different ways to get to the same place. People of affairs are paid merely to get there, thus creating the almost certain likelihood that when they do, they'll think that's the only way to do it—even when their neighbors got there by a different route.

But on this score, people of affairs are scarcely unique. How many times have you heard famous novelists describe the "right way" to work? Sit down and get started, don't wait for inspiration; write when you're ready, not when the schedule says so; write from dawn till noon; write from dusk till dawn; always write in the same place; never stick to the same place for long; write only about what you know, don't invent; only invent, all else is mere confession. Obviously, the expert at doing things is not very reliably expert in either understanding what he does or why it works, and certainly not in giving consistently good advice.

As a practicing certified academic who's paid, however paltry the sum, to think [There is this ancient conviction, firmly shared by taxpayers, trustees, and parents, against centuries of contrary evidence, that when it comes to professors, money corrupts, and therefore the less they get the purer their thoughts and the deeper their wisdom] as an academic, I will not profane the outdated professorial eccentricity of delivering of myself a peck of peccadillos illustrating the confusion and barrenness of the executive mind.

THE SUCCESS OF LARGE CORPORATIONS

The fact is, the executive mind is in very good condition indeed, especially in the larger and, usually therefore, multinational corporations. Indeed, awesome admiration is what any intelligent and fair-minded analyst will come away with when he studies the large corporation of our times, when he notes its extraordinary efficiency, flexibility, agility, internal diversity, the dedication and remarkable good spirits of its vast variety of employees, its attention to quality in what it does, fairness in how it behaves, and the studiousness with which it approaches major undertakings. Notwithstanding all the self-righteousness parading of unpleasant contrary facts these days, no institution of size or diversity, whether government or private, can on any reasonable combination of desirable attributes come within even modestly measurable distance of the large corporations of the modern capitalist democracies. Nor is this merely a matter of their having gotten a head start historically. *Fortune's* list of "Top 500" U.S. manufacturing corporations changes constantly, as does the list of top financial institutions. Federal Trade Commission studies of industrial concentration repeatedly show the shifting patterns of leadership in one industry sector after another.

Capitalism Works Better

Obviously, being ahead, or having gotten a head start, counts for not a lot within America's little corner of the capitalist world. But the parallel fact that everywhere the capitalist corporations, as a group, are widening their lead over their lagging imitators in the noncapitalist world is therefore extraordinarily significant. It means that being capitalistic gives them a genetic edge. Capitalism simply works better, and anybody who argues the opposite does just that. He argues. He simply doesn't have the facts.

One of the most interesting of these facts is the one which shows that those who seek to catch up with the more advanced and achieving institutions of our times invariably seek to do it by some sort of selective imitation of the modern capitalist corporations. ("We'll take your best and ignore the rest.") There is no traffic in the opposite direction, except for basketweaving and the fine art of producing illegal narcotics. Nothing could be more unmistakably meaningful. Nothing is more flattering of capitalism's protean prowess.

Even where imitations now have a long history, having been generously helped with facilitating patents, designs, machines, control systems, technicians-on-loan, cash, whole factories supplied by the capitalist corporations— as they have in Soviet Russia ever since Lenin's New Economic Policy first imported Henry Ford to build tractors in 1923—even when helped with the latest methods and technologies, the beneficiaries quickly fall behind again into inefficiency, sloth, and irrelevance. Why, one must ask, after over half a century of eager (if grudging) imitation and gifts of capitalist technologies in the factories and on the farms have the Soviets fallen with uncomprehending frustration ever further behind? Even their much vaunted advanced fighter plane that recently defected to Japan turned out to be advanced only in its packaging. (At least they learned *that* much from us—the importance of packaging.) This constant failure of helpful imitation to take hold, holds also in nations with feudal military dictatorships and in the false democracies of South America, Southeast Asia, and now of deimperialized Africa.

By what magic do the large corporations of the capitalist democracies work so well? Is it simply that they're capitalist, that they operate in democratic political environments, or some combination of the two? Or what?

The combination is crucial, emphatically. The corporations being capitalist means the liberating absence of the feudal incubus, traditions that fetter people to their assigned masters rather than binding them to their own chosen purposes. Their operating in political democracies means the likelihood of some sensible public resistance to any constantly advancing governmentalization of society, some reasonable probabilities against a constantly expanding and therefore suffocating bureaucratization of the entire polity. (It is instructive, I think, to note that no dictatorship or tyranny has ever been voted in by the people. People, however humble, however limited their educations, quite naturally and sensibly resist Caesarism, however elegantly it may be packaged or differently presented.)

Nor is it any more presumed to be a reactionary cliché to say these things, as it once was in Western liberal intellectual circles. The cliché has now become the dismal, tragic truth. The firm belief by generations of intelligent and informed idealists that justice and equality could be joined in symbiotic social conjugality via the attending ministrations of public servants working with diligent selflessness at control central has come a crushing cropper. It's now obvious that the future simply has not worked—not for Robert Owen, or Karl Marx, Rosa Luxemburg or Sydney and Beatrice Webb, Rexford Guy Tugwell, or Oscar Lange, or even for Fidel Castro or Lyndon Baines Johnson.

What seems somehow to work best is something we call private enterprise and the free market system of economic organization operating in a political environment we define and call "representative democracy."

Unfortunately, this explanation is not the whole of it. As we have seen, though business enterprises in the modern capitalist democracies as a group outperform all other such enterprises operating under different conditions of political and economic organization, we also saw that the distribution of this superiority is not symmetrical. Some firms lag, wither, and even die. Some prosper more than others. As I've suggested, the explanations of the superior performance that we most commonly get from the most successful practitioners of capitalist enterprise—though perhaps quite true and accurate in themselves—are seldom more than ordinary confessions of particular experiences, absent of comparison with the experiences of others, and devoid of serious analytical content. What they lack, moreover, in generality they often compensate with pomposity.

Requisites of Competitive Success

Professors also know something of the ways of pomposity, and especially of literary obfuscation masquerading as wisdom.

The genuine wisdom they have told in the past about the special reasons why reasonably free capitalist enterprises operating in reasonably open markets vary in performance, and what particular characteristics are associated with varying degrees of failure and success—that wisdom is, in fact, of relatively recent origin. It says essentially only the following few simple things about the requisites of success:

1. The purpose of an enterprise is to create and keep a customer.
2. To do that you have to produce and deliver goods and services that people want and value at prices and under conditions that are reasonably attractive relative to those offered by others to a proportion of customers large enough to make those prices and conditions possible.
3. To continue to do that, the enterprise must produce revenue in excess of costs in sufficient abundance and with sufficient regularity to attract, keep, and develop capital for the enterprise, and to keep at least abreast and sometimes ahead of competitive offerings.
4. No enterprise, no matter how small, can do any of this by mere instinct or accident. It has to clarify its purposes, strategies, and plans, and the larger the enterprise the greater the necessity that these be clearly written down, clearly communicated, and frequently reviewed by the senior members of the enterprise.
5. And in all cases, there must be an appropriate system of rewards, audits, and controls to assure that what's intended gets properly done, and when not, that it gets quickly rectified.

It was not so long ago that a lot of companies assumed something quite different about their purpose: They said quite simply that the purpose is to make money. But that proved as vacuous as to say that the purpose of life is to eat. Eating is a requisite, not a purpose of life. Without eating, life stops. Profits are a requisite of business. Without profits, business stops. Like food for the body, profit for the business must be defined as the excess of what goes in over what comes out. In business, it's called *positive cash flow*. It has to be positive because the process of sustaining life is a process of destroying life. To sustain life, a business must produce goods and services that people will, in sufficient numbers, want to buy at adequate prices. Since production wears out the machinery that produces and the people who run and manage the machines, to keep the business going there's got to be enough left over to replace what's being worn out. That "enough" is profit, no matter what the accountants, the IRS, or the Gosplan call it. That's why profit is a requisite, not a purpose of business.

Besides all that, to say that profit is a purpose of business is, simply, morally shallow. Who with an audible heartbeat and moderate sensibilities will go to the mat for the right of somebody to earn a profit for its own sake? If no greater purpose can be discerned or justified, business cannot, morally, justify its existence. It's a repugnant idea, an idea whose time has gone.

Finally, it's an empty idea. Profits can be made in lots of devious and transient ways. For people of affairs, a statement of purpose should provide guidance to the management of their affairs. To say that they should attract and hold customers forces them to figure out what people really want and value, and then to cater to those wants and values. It provides specific guidance and has moral merit.

Something over twenty years ago this new way of thinking about the business purpose led the more enlightened businesses slowly to distinguish operationally between marketing and selling, just as they also now distinguish between budgeting and planning, between long-range planning and strategic planning, between personnel management and human resources planning, between accounting and finance, between profit and cash flow, between the expected rate of return on investment and the present value of that expected rate of return.

All these are remarkably recent notions—few more than a generation old—developed mostly in our own lifetime. The most effective enterprises tend generally to practice them most conscientiously. They make a difference.

But of all these, the most powerful is the idea of marketing and the marketing view of the business process: that the purpose of a business is to create and keep a customer. There can be no corporate strategy that is not in some fundamental fashion a marketing strategy, no purpose that does not respond somehow to what people are willing to buy for a price. An asset consists of its capacity to generate revenue, either directly by its sale or the sale of what it helps, finally, to produce. Even a quick opportunistic raid on Wall Street has an underlying marketing rationale—that there's unrecognized or potential value greater than presently seen by others. The value is the asset, and that consists of its revenue-generating capability.

Indeed, those who so generally presume themselves furthest removed from the unsavory business of sales and marketing are often its most ardent practitioners. One needs only to observe the constantly competitive jockeying among Wall Street firms for exactly where their names appear on the printed syndication lists of underwritings. Why, if not for its future revenue-producing value, does so much genteel intrigue occupy the time of such self-consciously proper investment bankers? Even more telling is the Wall Street

assumption about the importance of flattery and obsequiousness in its relations with gigantic corporate customers. Special brass-plated, unnumbered
side doors quietly usher in the impressionable bigwigs of especially sought-
after investment banking accounts. Heavily starched linen tablecloths, Water-
ford crystal, and imported chefs once apprenticed to Paul Bocuse, character-
ize the opulent private dining rooms from which clients and prospective
clients may enjoy spectacular well-deserved views of the bustling city far
down below. The packaging by means of which investment banking firms
present themselves to their clients gets all the concentrated care that goes into
such other comparably hustled products as toiletries for the teeming masses.

Both practices endure because both work. Both customers buy hopeful expectations, not actual things. The ability to satisfy those expectations is more
effectively communicated by the packaging than by the simple generic
description of what's in the package. Feelings are more important than feeling. How we feel about a car is more important than how it feels. And so it
should be, especially when we consider that in the most important decisions of
life such as marriage, for example, we mostly decide not on the basis of the
cold figures in our intended's balance sheet, but our warm feelings about our
intended's figure.

There is, however, a problem. Most of you will recognize that I have been
talking about and praising "The Marketing Concept," an explicit reference I
have until now avoided only with enormous self-control. Even more self-control has attended any reference to "Marketing Myopia."[1] In that particular
manifesto, marketing was elevated to a kind of corporate consciousness-rais-
ing. It asserted the purposely narrow proposition that all energies should be
directed towards satisfying the consumer, no matter what. The rest, given reasonable good sense, would take care of itself. Nine years later, the manifesto
having done its intended work, I offered a more conciliatory and sensible
proposition: "The Marketing Matrix."[2] It incorporated some of the more
broadly based wisdom about the corporate purpose that I've implied today:
specifically, the need to balance, at some acceptable level of risk, the conditions of the external environment (customers, competition, government, and
society) with the conditions of the internal environment (resources, compe-
tences, options, and wishes).

In "The Marketing Matrix," I assert that early decline and certain death
are the fate of companies whose policies are geared totally and obsessively to
their own convenience at the total expense of the customer. (The last of some
twenty-five examples offered to describe such companies was: "In setting
your company goals, always set the standard in terms of production volume,

revenues, profits, and expanded stockholder equity. Never state them also in terms of market factors, customer-need fulfillment, customer-service objectives, or market targets.") In the matrix, the first part of this quoted example, ranked "9" on a nine-point scale of policies oriented entirely to the convenience of the company. The second part of this quoted example ("Never state them also in terms of market factors, customer need fulfillment. . . ." et cetera), ranked "1" on a nine-point scale of policies oriented to the customer. This was, in short a "9,1" company. There were examples also of "1,9" companies, "5,5" companies, and "9,9" companies. (The last were hard to find, and as hard to imagine. Nobody can be *that* virtuous, not even under expert professorial guidance.)

The problem with the marketing concept was half suggested in my chapter, "The Limits of the Marketing Concept," which followed directly after the matrix chapter. I am now about to drop the other shoe and suggest what is wrong with the remaining half.

MARKETS FACE CONSTANT CHANGE

The world of competitive enterprises openly facing each other in open markets is clearly a world of constant change. The marketing concept alerts us to this fact with the prescriptive injunction that to keep up requires studying, and responding to, what people want and value, quickly adjusting to choices provided by competitors. And it alerts us especially to the fact that competition often comes from outside the industry in which it finally occurs. Deeply implanted in these ideas is the notion that nothing is more important than the customer. The customer is, once more, King.

Suddenly IBM says something that appears quite different: "Be product, not customer, oriented." Revlon appears to say "Run the company, not just run after the customer." And they're both obviously right. Being a "1,9" company (little company-oriented, very customer-oriented) doesn't really work, nor does being a "9,1" company. Ranking as "9,9" is probably impossible, and "5,5" is probably an invitation to get outflanked on all sides.

The problem with the marketing concept—like all concepts in business, laws in physics, theories in economics, and all philosophies and ideologies—is their persistent tendency towards rigidity. They get dogmatized, interpreted into constantly narrower and inflexible prescriptions. In the case of the marketing concept, this is especially dangerous because of marketing's centrality in shaping the purposes, strategies, and tactics of the entire organization.

There is not, and cannot be, any rigid and lasting interpretations of what the marketing concept means in the specific ways a company should operate at any given time. Consider the cases of IBM and others once again.

IBM: The Product and Customer Needs

In November 1976 IBM did a funny thing—not "ha ha" funny, but "strange" funny. It finally unveiled its first venture into the world of minicomputers, now officially called Series/1. It did precisely what "Marketing Myopia" said it should: if customers prefer something that competes with your own offering, it's much more sensible for you to give it to them than let competitors do it. It's better to participate in the destruction of your own market than let it all be done by others. "Creative destruction," I called it, stealing that ringing phrase from Joseph Schumpeter, who was safely in the grave.

IBM was not the first company to enter the commercial computer business. It was, in fact, a particularly late latecomer. But in what seemed like no time, it captured at least 80% of the mainframe segment of what, in 1976, was a $20 billion industry. IBM did so largely by being a singularly dedicated and spectacularly effective marketing company. Right through 1976, in its entire history this master symbol of modern science and technology has never had more than two senior executives who had not come up the organizational ladder primarily via the marketing route, and in that entire history, only one was a scientist. The master symbol of twentieth-century science and technology succeeded largely because of its marketing prowess, claims to the singular advantage imparted by the Forrester memory drum notwithstanding. It had industry managers who developed marketing plans, sales programs, and sales training for specifically targeted industries and companies. IBM salesmen were as specialized in the industries to which they were assigned to sell as in the hardware they offered for sale. The company bundled the software right into the product offering at a single set price, so that the customer was assured that the equipment would indeed be programmed to do the promised job. It designated installation facilities for the customer, redesigned his entire data collection and reporting systems, trained his data processing people, took the shakedown cruise, and then later developed new EDP applications to help the client even more. In the process, the client became an even bigger and more dependent customer. Meanwhile the customer had the option of paying the single nonnegotiable price either by paying outright for everything, or leasing it with virtually no punitive cancellation provisions. If ever there was a thoroughgoing marketing-oriented professional organization, it was IBM. And it worked like magic.

But in November 1976 with Series/1, all that was chucked. The Series/1 sales force was made product-oriented rather than customer- and application-oriented. It became a dedicated sales force—dedicated to selling Series/1 hardware and that's it. No special customer help. Sell, sell, sell to everybody on the pike. And no more leasing options. Cash on the barrelhead, that's all, in spite of the fact that IBM's easy financial capability of offering the lease option has long given it a powerful competitive edge.

Series/1 is clearly a case of creative destruction—competing with yourself in order to save yourself. Nothing really very new about that. But abandoning marketing, sales, and pricing practices that had proved so effective for almost totally opposite practices, *that's* new.

Just as successful managers and entrepreneurs who presume to give advice to all others on the basis of their own limited experiences are likely to give advice of limited relevance or utility, so do professors of business administration when their ideas become as rigid as other people's experiences. Series/1 switched to product-orientedness because conditions changed. In the Series/2 family (which is sure to come) customer- and application-orientedness may again become competitively appropriate.

In Series/1, as in its original entry into the computer business, the company was an imitator, a follower of others that preceded it by many years into the market with the product. But when the computer was a relatively new idea, its manufacturers knew a great deal more about its potential uses and usability than its potential users. The needs of potential users for the product had to be converted into wants. For wants to become purchases, the purchasers had to be carefully educated and guided to the product's uses. IBM had to educate its own sales people in the businesses to which they were to sell. All this was not so different from the creation of a mass market for eye shadow and eye liners just a decade ago. The big cosmetics houses had to establish demonstration counters in the stores to teach women how to use the product.

But once educated, either by the seller or by the mushrooming number of independent schools and courses available elsewhere as the markets expanded, the customer became able to make his own decisions about what he needed and how to use it. Thus the more successful the sellers became in teaching their prospects to want and use their products, the less dependent their users became on their sellers. In the first instance, "the product" being sold was a complex cluster of value satisfactions that included education, training, hands-on help, continuing advice, quick availability for emergency situations. Later, in maturity, as the customer became more sophisticated, "the product" by definition became much simpler. It became, if not exactly a commodity, certainly not a complex cluster of things. It became, simply, a computer, simply an elegant little dish of eye shadow.

But more, as the computer got involved in more things in the corporation (largely, at first, with the suggested help of its manufacturers, and later more and more with the help of internal specialists in the user organization), it became a hard-to-manage monster. different users within the organization made different and often conflicting demands on it. It became a continuing battle as to how to charge different departments and individuals for its use, and for the accompanying software, which proved increasingly more costly. All this finally created a market for the minicomputer. A corporate department, division, or even individual could now have his own small computer, programmed or programmable the way he wanted it. The invention of integrated circuits, and then microprocessors, turned a trickle into a flood.

With customers as sophisticated about the product as its sellers, with equipment costs low, and with strongly established competing sellers, the properly marketing-oriented thing for IBM to have done was precisely what it did: sell the simple hardware hard, absent of attendant beneficiating clusters of the past. And it worked, like magic.

Revlon and Management Methods

In November 1976, Business Week's lead article on Revlon had the following headline and subhead: "Management Realists in the Glamour World of Cosmetics: Flair and flamboyance yield to controls, budgets, planning." We all know enough to know from that what was in the article. We should also know that in the first year of an entirely new operating style, one that substituted management for mystique, sales rose 18% and profits 16%. Nine months into the next year sales were up another 23% and earnings 25%.

Who's to say that Revlon, no matter how big it gets, will be able now always to function effectively and prosperously under its new managerial dispensation? Maybe for some purposes miscegenation will become the mode. In the words of Richard Barrie, the new president of Faberge, Inc., "Somewhere along the line the industry has to shake off the old idea of management by mystique, yet still retain the mystique in its marketing." Who's to say?

As one finally lays down Andrew Tobias's book about the bizarre, coruscating career of Charles Revson, it is clear enough that towards the end Revson himself began to wonder about the fickle feudal terror with which he ran his empire.[3] His escalating *ad hominum* hatred of his competitors merely mirrored his uncertainties about his managerial methods. When, finally, after several shatteringly disastrous trials with managers of a different breed, he brought in Michel C. Bergerac, the elegant French-born head of International Telephone and Telegraph Corporation's European operations. When he brought in Bergerac, he set into motion at Revlon precisely the same kind of transformation that characterized Series/1. So urgently did Revson feel the need, that he paid Bergerac $1.5 million just for signing up with Revlon, added a five-year contract for a salary of $325,000. a year, and three-year options for 70,000 shares of stock.

The problem was that competition had become more professionalized, with some of the biggest cosmetics houses having been sold to drug and package-goods companies. The regulatory climate had become tougher. Distribution costs suddenly rose sharply, with competition making it harder to get compensating price rises. The tonnage of what moved out the factory gates suddenly became as crucial as the tone of its colors. Bergerac, whose continental suaveness assuaged Revlon's hard-eyed glamour merchants, also earned their respect for his ITT management methods. The merchandising tail no longer wagged so vigorously the management dog—just as things should be. And it worked, like magic.

Allegheny Ludlum Steel: Educating the Customer

Not so long ago stainless steel was a specialty steel. As with computers, customers had to be created by being taught and shown how to use it as well as what might be done to use it more abundantly—to give them as well a competitive edge in *their* markets. The most important part of "the product" in those early days was not the steel itself, but the design and application services provided by its chief manufacturer, Allegheny Ludlum Steel. Customers who were buying regular carbon steel, often more conveniently and in smaller quantities and with faster deliveries from local independent steel warehouses, now bought stainless steel quite willingly from the factory in larger quantities, with longer delivery times, and no price shadings. They needed the factory's help on other matters more than the local warehouses' convenience.

In time, however, the independent warehouse market share of stainless steel rose. Allegheny Ludlum lost market share to competitors who sold more intensively through such warehouses. Like IBM, having educated the customer, the customer no longer needed the supplier's attendant cluster of benefits—or, at least, less of them. Selling had to become less marketing oriented, in the traditional sense, and more vigorously product and sales oriented. The number of warehouses had to be expanded, or mill inventories expanded so as to speed up deliveries. In selling, "who you know" became relatively more important than "what you know."

Allegheny Ludlum changed to a new mode. It cannot be said that it scuttled the marketing concept. Instead, it adopted a new version, a new marketing mode to deal with different needs and pressures. It did not ignore the customer, did not try to shove down his throat what he did not want. It merely simplified and streamlined "the product" to the customer's new specifications. The marketing concept remained in healthy charge—except now it called for something different than what was becoming, in some places, a rigidly dogmatized version of what it should be. And it worked, like magic.

Chevrolet and Product Identity

Take, on the other hand, Chevrolet at General Motors. To read Alfred P. Sloan Jr.'s autobiographical *My Years With General Motors,* the advice one walks away with about how to run a successful company includes the idea that each item in the corporate product line should have a clearly distinctive identity, even though all the products are generically the same. "A car is a car," but not really. A Chevrolet is actually a low-priced entrée car, built for youthful peppiness yet roomy enough for new-family practicality. Next comes the Pontiac step-up, a clear rise on the ladder of its owner's maturity and success. The larger, sturdier, more impressive Buick is for the solidly achieving middle manager, solidly on the road to better things. The Oldsmobile confirms the attainment of those better things, and the Cadillac of the best things. Everybody knows clearly who the car is for and exactly what its possession signifies.

But for nearly two decades Chevrolet has now successfully violated Sloan's sacred dictums. Its *own* line of cars is itself wider than the entire General Motors line during Sloan's remarkably successful tenure as its chief executive officer. And it is wider not simply in the sizes and prices of its cars, and the options it offers the customers for them, but it even has more brand names of its own than Sloan ever had for the entire corporation. Meanwhile, all General Motors divisions have expanded their lines (up and down) across each other's turfs, and still the Chevrolet division prospers more than ever, as does the entire corporation. And there's not the slightest whiff of evidence that it's a fragile castle built up momentarily on or out of sand.

Only a fool would argue that Chevrolet is not market-oriented, or that General Motors is confused or has gone berserk. Certainly Alfred Sloan would approve, though his book implies the opposite. His book was written for times when cars were more important as symbols of attainment or expressions of aspirations. As the customer has changed, so has General Motors. And it's worked, like magic.

Exxon and Gulf: Two Approaches To Marketing Gasoline

Finally, contrast Exxon and Gulf in the late 1950s for final proof that not even the luck of sudden riches from beneath the Arabian sands can save one from the necessity of doing things right. Gulf, at that time the biggest beneficiary of all, opted for quick conversion of oil into cash. It vastly expanded its service-station network throughout the United States, leasing new lands for grand new stations, and just as fast leasing marginal old stations in declining places. It even created a subregular grade of gasoline, Gulftane, to be sold along with regular and supreme, for a penny less than regular.

Exxon opted for the opposite. It stuck to a policy of careful new-site selection and systematic elimination of older and declining stations. It began to buy the land and buildings of its service stations, thus balancing one type of expanding fixed asset in distant lands with another type at home where land values were on a secular rise. Moreover, owning rather than leasing its retail outlets made it easier to modify them to the specifications with which it sought to attract more customers per outlet. It worked harder at selecting and training its service station attendants. And, though like Gulf, it also acquired many more stations, it did so by buying not individual stations, but entire companies that were specifically in the retail gasoline vending business. These Exxon upgraded and gradually shifted over to its own brand.

Long before October 1973, when suddenly oil in the ground nearly quadrupled in value, and even before increasing ownership participation and expropriation by the Arab countries had reduced the share of what was physically left in the ground, it became apparent to Gulf that it had made a major error. It proved more costly to sell cheap crude in small and declining stations than more costly crude in larger more efficient ones. That discovery was foretold long before by others. But what proved more costly than these expenses alone was the attendant destruction of customers. In this case, as opposed to General Motors, expanding the line downward (Exxon expanded it upward with a superpremium) and expanding the types of stations and locations produced both confusion within Gulf and among its customers. What little serious brand preference there was among major-brand gasoline buyers almost totally vanished for Gulf. With the greatest cost in money and human spirit within the corporation, Gulf has for a decade now been trying to undo and redo what it did so fast in just a few years before.

In the 1950s, it suddenly *did* become obsessively product-oriented. And it worked, like magic, in the wrong direction.

THE MARKET CALLS THE TUNE

These examples tell us something we all know but don't always practice in our thoughts and actions: that to refer to an organization's principal marketing policies and strategies is to refer to that organization's principal overall corporate policies and strategies; that its principal overall corporate policies and strategies cannot be shaped absent of serious marketing considerations; that there are stages in the evolution of markets that may require policies and strategies which appear, falsely on the surface, perversely product-oriented; but that in all this variation and adjustment and oscillation there must be persistent, remorseless, unforgiving, overriding orderliness and logic, no matter how much things seem to be different or to change. This overriding orderliness and logic is the logic of the marketing concept. The market calls the tune, and the players better play it right.

CONCLUSION

Popular philosophy treats us often to seemingly contradictory advice: "Nothing is so constant as change"; "The more things change, the more they remain the same."

If either can be, can both be? If both can be, can either be?

Popular philosophy is often popular because it makes so much sense to so many. And though on many things the many are often wrong, they rarely remain wrong for long. Unlike professors and ideologues, the rest do not cling for long with casuistry or obsessive ardor to ideas or dogmas that don't work.

Look at our solar system, and the constantly changing configuration of the planets around the sun. Up there there is nothing so constant as change. Look again. After 365 changing days, the earth repeats with predictable regularity the same precise pattern as before. And so, in their own cycles, do all the other planets and their satellites. The more things change, the more they remain the same. If either can be, both can be. If both can be, either can also be.

And so when men of affairs presume in their twilight years to tell all others "how to do it" by telling merely how *they* happen to have done it, they may be right for their particular one three-hundred-sixty-fifth day of the year, but not necessarily for the remaining three hundred sixty-four. It may be that it takes a Copernicus or a Kepler to study the entire whole in order for the rest of us to understand the underlying order, the constants that the daily pressures of events keep us from recognizing as constants. Down there in the competitive ring, things seldom look as panoramically clear as up in the stands where the observers sit in disembodied comfort.

But the fact that they can't be *seen* by them in the ring so well, does not suggest that what they say is any less true. Certainly it will be more keenly felt. Nothing is as bracing or as certain as what is directly experienced. In my book, *The Marketing Mode,* I placed the following words from Robert Graves on the dedication page:

> Experts ranked in serried rows
> Filled the enormous plaza full
> But only one is there who knows
> And he's the man who fights the bull.

It was meant, in spite of the 345 pages of self-assured academic text that followed, as an expression of respect and admiration for the fundamental wisdom of people of affairs, the practitioners out there who fight the bull. What they experience and feel in the difficult life of directing and managing organizations has to be respected. Only *they* know how it feels, but they know only how it feels in *their* particular circumstances and only from the angle of vision provided them *down there* on the turf. Up here in the stands we know little of how it feels, but perhaps a lot about how it looks, especially as compared with all the others down there on the turf. And from this comparison it is possible, though generally difficult, to know also what it means.

I see a constant that defines the best. It says that there is a structural link between free and open markets and free and open societies; that economic development prospers best where there can be institutions that can freely act on the understanding that they can have no effective strategy that is not marketing oriented—that is, that does not in some sensibly conscious fashion monitor and respond to reasonably free and open markets. From this there follows this unyielding prescript: The purpose of enterprise is to create and keep a customer. To do that, you have to do those things that will make people *want* to do business with you. All other truths on this subject are merely derivative.

NOTES

1. Theodore Levitt, "Marketing Myopia," *Harvard Business Review* (July-August 1960) and (September-October 1975).
2. In Theodore Levitt, *The Marketing Mode* (New York: McGraw-Hill, 1969), Chapter 11.
3. Andrew Tobias, *Fire and Ice: The Story of Charles Revson, The Man Who Built the Revlon Empire* (New York: Morrow, 1976).

THREE

Marketing's Drive to Maturity

Philip Kotler

Harold T. Martin Professor of Marketing
Northwestern University

The following observations can be made about the evolution, status, and future of marketing:

1. The marketing function is unevenly represented in different industries today. It entered certain industries early, others late, and still others not at all.
2. Insufficient demand is the key factor that sparks a firm's or industry's initial interest in marketing.
3. Marketing is normally resisted when introduced into a firm and it must fight an uphill battle to establish its role and scope.
4. As marketing takes roots in the firm, it becomes recognized as increasingly crucial to the firm's future growth and survival.
5. Marketing, however, passes through several stages of misconception in the firm before it is correctly understood and applied.
6. In time, and especially with success, companies tend to forget some of their basic marketing principles and a continuous reeducation effort is necessary to fight marketing regression.
7. Although undermarketing describes the state of marketing in most industries, cases of overmarketing are beginning to appear.
8. Marketing's major task in the next decade will be to adjust its philosophies and strategies toward greater consonance with societal and environmental concerns.

BUSINESS FUNCTIONS IN BALANCE

Organizations require a well-balanced mix of inputs to survive and grow. Companies require money, manpower, materials, machines, and markets— the five M's. The required ratios of these inputs vary over time and space. But it is possible for a company to concentrate excessively on some inputs over others. It is common to find companies, for example, with a technological fixation. They invent better mousetraps, only to discover the lack of customers. Other companies are production fixated. They concentrate their energies trying to figure out ways to lower the costs of producing a staple item and overlook the fact that the staple item is about to be displaced in the market by something better. The telltale sign of management function fixation is the emergence of formidable problems created by the neglect of certain functions. A company whose costs are rising faster than competitors' costs may be neglecting production in favor of some other functions. A company with high customer turnover may be neglecting the marketing function. The challenge is to detect the imbalance before a serious malfunctioning breaks out. A periodic audit is desirable to see whether a company is striking a good balance among the inputs that will count in its success.

Whether a firm is investing sufficient resources in marketing is not simply measured by its budget for advertising, field sales, marketing research, and customer service. A company could be spending a lot on marketing and still not enough, and another company can be spending a little on marketing and yet too much. A further complication is that marketing is a two-tiered function in companies. Marketing is both a specialized function and a top management function. A company can overinvest in the specialized marketing function and underinvest in the top marketing function—or the reverse.

THE ORIGINS OF MARKETING

As a concept, marketing is not very old. The question "How old is marketing?" always brings forth quaint answers. Some people date marketing as beginning with earliest man, and go so far as to call it "the world's oldest profession." Some even say marketing predates man. Consider the following argument for subspecie marketing:

> I do not think it would be stretching the point too far to say that the reproductive cycle of plants is a natural exchange for profit system.

After all, a flower, with its colour and perfume, is an advertisement for nectar. The exchange deal is quite straightforward—the bee has the nectar in return for pollen it has picked up elsewhere and for taking that flower's pollen onto the next one. At the next stage of the cycle the colour and perfume of the fruit is an advertisement for food. The bird eats the fruit and distributes the seeds in return.[1]

Others advance the argument that marketing began when mankind first engaged in exchange, that is, when two parties with surpluses resorted to barter as an alternative to employing force, stealing, or begging to obtain goods. Barter evolved into the fine art of selling which received high expression in very early civilizations.

However, marketing is not selling, and therefore marketing is a much newer idea. In fact, we must date marketing's beginning in the early twentieth century! One criterion for the beginning of a field of study is its emergence into academic consciousness. The term *marketing* was first used in course titles in the early 1900s. In 1905, W. E. Kreusi taught a course at the University of Pennsylvania entitled "The Marketing of Products."[2]In 1910, Ralph Starr Butler offered a course entitled "Marketing Methods" at the University of Wisconsin. Butler explained how he conceived marketing:

> In considering the whole field of selling I developed the idea that personal salesmanship and advertising had to do simply with the final expression of the selling idea. My experience with the Procter & Gamble Company had convinced me that a manufacturer seeking to market a product had to consider and solve a large number of problems before he ever gave expression to the selling idea by sending a salesman on the road or inserting an advertisement in a publication.
>
> I surveyed the very meager literature of business which was available at that time and was astonished to find that the particular field that I have very briefly described above had never been treated by any writer.[3]

The crystallization of marketing can also be dated by attempting to establish when marketing departments were first installed in companies. Sales departments, of course, have a long history reaching back into the nineteenth and earlier centuries. Drucker dates the start of marketing in the West in the middle nineteenth century at the International Harvester Company.

> The first man in the West to see marketing clearly as the unique and central function of the business enterprise, and the creation of a custom-

er as the specific job of management, was Cyrus H. McCormick (1809-84). The history books mention only that he invented a mechanical harvester. But he also invented the basic tools of modern marketing: market research and market analysis, the concept of market standing, pricing policies, the service salesman, parts and service supply to the customer, and installment credit. He had done all this by 1850, but not till fifty years later was he first widely imitated even in his own country.[4]

Yet International Harvester did not establish a marketing department as such; rather it had an enlightened sales department. Marketing departments had their roots in the development of marketing research in the early twentieth century. The Curtis Publishing Company is credited with installing in 1911 the first marketing research department (called "commercial research" at the time) under the direction of Charles Coolidge Parlin. Marketing research departments were subsequently established in U.S. Rubber (1916) and Swift and Company (1917).[5] These departments were viewed as adjuncts to the sales department. Their task was to develop information that would make it easier for sales departments to sell. Over time, marketing research departments accepted additional responsibilities such as sales analysis and marketing administration. Some time later, companies began to combine marketing research, advertising, customer services, and other miscellaneous marketing functions into marketing departments.

Marketing departments appeared in industrial equipment firms, consumer equipment firms, and consumer packaged goods firms—in somewhat this order—although the evidence is scant. Marketing moved most rapidly as an idea into those industries and companies afflicted with insufficient or falling demand. These companies were ready to consider any approach offering to help boost their sales volume.

HOSTILITY TOWARD MARKETING

Yet marketing was rarely greeted with open arms. Entrenched company interests in the form of financial and production executives saw marketing as a disreputable bag of tricks or as a threat to their power and status. Some of the early marketers may have contributed to this by their aggressiveness or overclaiming. In any event, marketing crowded and challenged the other business functions. The company marketers argued that production should adjust to the needs of the marketplace rather than requiring the marketplace to adjust

(a) Traditional View

(b) Transitional View

(c) Druckerian View

Fig. 3.1   EVOLVING CONCEPTIONS OF BUSINESS

to the interests of production. And marketers argued that financial officers could not apply tests of current profitability to all marketing expenditures because these expenditures created long run goodwill and market penetration. Slowly, and not without bitter battles, the marketer's arguments won out. Originally, the sales-marketing function was seen as one of several, equally important business functions in a checks-and-balances relationship as shown in Fig. 3.1(a). Later, the dearth of demand resulted in territorial encroachments by sales-marketing at the expense of other functions as illustrated by Fig. 3.1(b). More recently, some companies have adopted the Druckerian view that "marketing is so basic that it cannot be considered a separate function. . . . It is the whole business seen from the point of view of its final result, that is, from the customer's point of view"[6]; see Fig. 3.1(c). Thus, the other business functions are correct in recognizing that a strong marketing orientation might reduce their relative power within the company.

The threat potential of marketing as it enters new industries is illustrated currently in the newspaper industry where one newspaper editor recently wrote a diatribe entitled "Beware the 'Market' Thinkers."[7] This editor warned newspapers not to let marketers in because they do not understand the function of newspapers, which is to print news. Marketing is not the solution, he feels, to the national decline in newspaper readership. Marketers would corrupt all that is good about today's newspapers.

FURTHER DIFFUSION OF MARKETING

Once marketing successfully established itself in industrial and consumer goods firms, marketing champions began to emerge in some consumer service industries. Marketing did not get far in the railroad industry but did come in swiftly and effectively in the airline industry. Airlines began to study travellers' attitudes toward different features of their service—schedule frequency, baggage handling, in-flight service, friendliness, seat comfort. It was not long afterward that airlines shed the notion they were in the air carrier business and began to operate on the insight that they were in the total travel business. The next service industry to flirt with marketing was the banking industry. Bankers showed great resistance to marketing ideas but in the end capitulated. Marketing is beginning to invade the insurance industry and the stock brokerage industry, although marketing is still poorly understood in these industries.

The most recent invasion of marketing has been in the nonprofit sector of the economy. Such disparate organizations as colleges, hospitals, police departments, museums, and symphonies are currently flirting with marketing. Marketing is at different stages of attention in these various industries. The U.S. Army, Navy, and Marines have welcomed marketing as their major hope in filling their manpower needs in a zero-draft environment. American colleges and universities, troubled with declining enrollments, are eager to try out marketing ideas in their admissions operation. An increasing number of hospitals are beginning to look seriously into marketing as their bed counts go down. As a sign of the times, the Evanston Hospital of Evanston, Illinois, recently appointed the world's first vice president of marketing for a hospital.

BANKING: A CASE STUDY

Although marketing fought its way into many industries, it entered without proper understanding. Both its proponents and opponents have tended to confuse marketing with one of its subfunctions, particularly advertising or selling. Marketing enlightenment grows slowly in a company and tends to pass through several stages. The stages are described below in the context of the banking industry.

Initially, banks had no understanding or regard for marketing. Virtually all banks before the middle 1950s regarded themselves as above marketing. Banks were supplying needed services. They did not have to demonstrate the need for checking accounts, savings, loans, or safety deposit boxes. Banks followed certain simple rules in their customer relations. First, they should not loan money to many who really need it. Second, the customer should feel awe when dealing with a bank. Everything about banks before the fifties was calculated to make the customer recognize that he was visiting a Greek temple and paying homage to the gods. I remember hearing about a bank loan officer who arranged his office so that a potential borrower would sit across from his massive desk on a lower chair than his own. The window in the office was located behind the officer's back and the sun would pour in on the hapless customer as he would try to explain why he needed a loan. This was the bank's posture before the age of marketing.

Marketing Is Advertising, Sales Promotion, and Publicity

Marketing came into banks in the late 1950s, not in the form of the marketing concept but in the form of the "Advertising and Promotion Concept."

Banks and other financial institutions were experiencing increased competition for savings. A few buccaneer financial institutions decided to adopt the marketing tools of the soap companies. They "lowered" their professional standards—according to their critics—and adopted the ways of the "huckster" and "pitchman." Their offers of "pots and pans" succeeded, however, in attracting new customers. Their competitors were forced into adopting the same measures and scurried out to hire advertising agencies and promotion experts.

Marketing Is Smiling and Friendly Atmosphere

The banks that first introduced modern advertising and promotion soon found their advantage cancelled by the rush of imitators. They also learned another lesson: attracting people to a bank is easy; converting them to loyal customers is hard. These banks began to formulate a larger concept of marketing, that of trying to please the customer. Bankers had to learn to smile. The tellers had to be retrained. The bars had to be taken off the tellers' windows. The interior of the bank had to be redesigned to produce a warm, friendly atmosphere. Even the outside Greek Temple architecture had to be changed. Bank atmospheres became the battleground of competition.

The first banks to implement this insight soon began to outperform their competitors in attracting and holding new customers. However, their competitors quickly figured out what was happening and rushed into programs of institutionalizing thoroughgoing friendliness. Soon all banks became so friendly that it was impossible for a customer to find a "no-nonsense bank." As a competitive attribute, friendliness became so widespread that it lost its potency as a primary factor in bank choice.

Marketing Is Innovation

Banks then had to search for a new exploitable basis for differential advantage. Those who read Professor Levitt's article on "Marketing Myopia"[8] began to realize that marketing transcended advertising and friendliness, although these were important ingredients. Banks were not narrowly in the savings business: they were in the business of meeting the evolving and varied financial needs of customers. These banks began to think in terms of conducting a program of continuous innovation where they assume leadership in identifying and introducing new customer services: credit cards, Christmas savings plans, automatic bank loans, and so on. Some banks took this so seriously that, like the First National Bank of Chicago, they now offer over 350 financial products to customers. Successful innovation provides a competitive lead to the innovative bank. However, financial products are easily copied and advantages are short-lived. But, if the innovator routinizes innovation, then it is continuously ahead of other banks in its area.

Marketing Is Positioning

What happens when a number of leading banks all advertise, smile, and innovate? Clearly they begin to look alike again. Again they search for a new dimension of marketing and discover "positioning." No bank can be the best bank for all services. A bank cannot innovate all products and serve all customers with equal effectiveness. A bank must choose. It must review its best opportunities and "take a position" in the market.

Positioning is a competitive marketing tool that goes beyond image-making. The image-making bank seeks to cultivate an image in the customer's mind that it is a large bank or a friendly bank or an efficient bank. It often develops a symbol like the Harris lion or the Continental kangaroo to personify this virtue in a distinctive way. Yet the customer may still see the competing banks as basically alike, except for the chosen symbols. Positioning is an attempt to distinguish the bank from its competitors along real dimensions in order to be the most preferred bank by the subset of the market looking for that type of bank. Positioning aims to help a customer know the real differences between competing banks so that he can choose more efficiently in terms of his financial requirements. Some bank marketers feel that the positioning step is the ultimate expression of modern bank marketing. This, of course, is not the case.

Marketing Is Analysis, Planning, and Control

There is a higher concept of bank marketing that represents the ultimate essence of modern marketing. The issue is whether the bank has installed systems for marketing analysis, planning, and control. One large bank, which had achieved sophistication in the previous dimensions of advertising, friendliness, innovation, and positioning, nevertheless lacked meaningful systems of marketing planning and control. For example, each year the commercial loan officers submitted to management their volume goal, usually a figure 10 to 15% higher than the current year volume. They also requested a budget increase of 10 to 15%. No rationale or plans accompanied these submissions. Bank management was satisfied with its officers who achieved their goals. One loan officer—judged to be a good performer-retired and was replaced by a younger man who proceeded to increase the loan volume 50% the following year! The bank painfully learned that it had been failing to measure the potential of its various markets; it had failed to require marketing plans, to set quotas, and to develop motivation and reward systems.

LAW OF SLOW LEARNING

Thus, these financial institutions demonstrated a "law of slow learning" with regard to grasping the revolutionary character of marketing. This pattern seems to be repeated as marketing enters each new industry. Colleges are currently excited about marketing but they see it mainly as an advertising and promotion function located within the admissions office. They do not think of it in terms of improving the warmth of their institutions, innovating new programs, positioning themselves more clearly, or installing systems of marketing analysis, planning, and control.

The interesting question is whether organizations must go through these slow stages to learn their marketing or whether they can come to it fully. The plain truth is that each stage is so revolutionary in its potential for volume buildup as well as internal disruption that perhaps institutions are wise in coming to terms with marketing one step at a time. As each stage is installed and proves itself, it makes the company environment more receptive to further advance in marketing consciousness and practice.

There are three alternative approaches to explaining marketing to those who oppose its introduction into an organization. The traditional approach is to describe marketing as a promotion force that will lead to healthy increases in company sales. A second approach is to describe marketing as the systematic study of market needs and market opportunities in order to develop better products, prices, distribution, and promotion. A third approach goes to the extreme of saying that marketing is not selling and advertising but in fact their opposite. According to Drucker, "the aim of marketing is to make selling superfluous. The aim of marketing is to know and understand the customer so well that the product or service fits him and sells itself."[9]

LAW OF FAST FORGETTING

Even after marketing is installed in an organization and matures through the various stages, management must fight a strong tendency to forget basic marketing principles. Management tends to forget marketing in the wake of its success. Some large American companies plunged into the European market, refusing to note the many differences between and within European nations and to modify their products, communications, and distribution concepts. In many cases, their product entries ended in disaster. Sorenson noted:

> In the United States, the marketing concept appears to be well into the mature phase of its own life cycle. It is increasingly being questioned, criticized, and—in some instances—ignored or discarded. By contrast, the marketing concept in Europe is alive and vigorous and just entering the rapid growth stage of its life cycle.[10]

UNDERMARKETING

Marketing tends to enter new industries slowly, with inadequate understanding, and with tendencies toward forgetting. Most industries and firms today are still characterized by undermarketing which exists in a firm when top management has an inadequate comprehension of marketing and sees it simply as promotion or a set of specialized functions. To this extent, the firm is failing to realize the potential contribution of marketing toward clarifying the company's mission, identifying new products and market opportunities, and influencing strategic planning.

Undermarketing also occurs when the firm fails to budget adequate marketing money to achieve corporate objectives. The following example is not untypical:

> An industrial equipment manufacturer with $55 million in sales budgets less than $500,000 for advertising and promotion. Since the firm sells many products, this budget is spread too thinly and fails to create much of an impact for any one product line. One of the company's divisions introduced five different major innovations into its industry and lost market leadership each time. The divisional manager, when asked why he did not spend more on marketing, replied that he is

responsible for current profitability and unfortunately the fruits of promotional spending do not all blossom in the current period.

OVERMARKETING

A firm, industry, or even a whole society can also be guilty of overmarketing. This possibility has not been recognized because until now, the problem
has been too little marketing rather than too much marketing. Overmarketing
develops when a firm, industry, or society begins to invest so much in marketing that other results and values are jeopardized.

Company Overmarketing

Overmarketing is well-illustrated by the case of a management consulting
firm that was founded in the mid-1940s with the objective of achieving sustained long-term growth.[11] The firm's management developed a long-range
plan based on the application of the following marketing principles:

1. Marketing was recognized as a company-wide activity with clearly defined areas of responsibility. Staff men and supervisors were
   expected to work on expanding services to existing clients; officers were expected to develop new clients and to close sales leads
   opened by the staff. The entire program was under the personal
   direction of the President.
2. There was a carefully planned and vigorous program for building
   referral sources. Each officer was required to belong to a different
   city club and was encouraged to belong to a country club. Bank
   contacts were pursued systematically as a source of leads. Officers
   were expected and staff men encouraged to fill speaking engage-
   ments or to write articles.
3. Frequent meetings were held to coordinate and plan new business
   development activities. Training sessions were conducted to improve new business development skills.
4. A public relations consultant was retained to obtain favorable
   newspaper and trade paper publicity. Publicity releases were prepared covering important company assignments. Seminars were
   held from time to time on important management techniques.
5. Every effort was made to motivate new business development ac-

tivity. Staff men were paid bonuses for successful leads. Ability to generate new business was made a significant element in promotion to supervisor and the major element in promotion to officer. Officers' compensation was based almost entirely on the volume and rate of growth of the client assignments under their supervision.

Over the short run this program produced outstanding results. By 1959, fee billings had risen to over $4 million a year from offices located in six major cities. However, this represented a high point from which the firm began a decline, at first slowly and then precipitously. As the fortunes of the company declined, the organization fell into disarray. All the branch offices were closed. Several officers resigned to establish their own consulting firms. At the present time, the original company is still in existence but is no longer a major competitor in its field.

The reversal of the company's fortunes was not the result of new factors or conditions in the marketplace. Rather the company paid a deferred penalty for long-term overemphasis on marketing. Having committed itself to a rapid growth goal, it neglected other things, specifically:

1. The original objective was for a sustained rate of growth of over 15% a year. This was achieved but the effort involved did not leave sufficient time for the acquisition, training, and development of the professional staff. The firm was developing business at a rate somewhat faster than it was developing the capacity to handle it.

2. This problem was exacerbated by the effects of the emphasis placed on new business development and the methods that were adopted to motivate it. Staff men perceived that high awards were given for business development, but not necessarily for professional excellence. A number of staff men of great professional promise, but little interest in selling, left the firm to join competitors. The multiplier effect of these resignations increased the difficulty of coordinating staff development with growth.

3. In view of the fact that officers were selected primarily for their ability to develop new business, they occasionally lacked the technical background to supervise properly the assignments handled by their own staff, who were more likely to have been selected on the basis of proven professional skills. The difference in compensation between officers and staff consultants was substantial, giving rise to poor morale, increasing the problem of turnover, and mak-

ing it impossible to give proper supervision to complex and important assignments.

4. The high financial rewards for new business development led to savage competition and infighting between company officers and contributed to an unhealthy atmosphere throughout the firm.

Thus a firm can overemphasize the job of marketing to the detriment of other important business functions. An intense passion for volume and growth can be at the expense of long-run profitability. Fortunately, firms are beginning to tie financial responsibility more closely into marketing. Company marketers are becoming more financial minded under the pressure of declining profits. They are increasingly formulating their goals and plans in terms of profits rather than sales volume.

Industry Overmarketing

Whole industries also may experience overmarketing. This situation develops where each firm is forced in self-defense to duplicate the expensive marketing practices of the marketing leaders. All firms become saddled with heavy marketing costs that must be passed on to customers. For years, the cigarette industry's advertising expenditures escalated each year to protect market shares, not to obtain market growth. No cigarette company could unilaterally cut its advertising and promotion budget without suffering dire consequences. Such an overmarketing stalemate could only be broken in one of two ways. One is for a market leader to de-escalate its expenditures, hoping the others will follow. The other is by law or regulation restricting certain types of marketing activities. When cigarette advertising on television and radio was banned, the industry enjoyed windfall profits which it used to diversify into other industries.

The issue of industry overmarketing is being discussed abroad more than in the United States. Various governments are taking steps to intervene in industry situations which they regard as showing excessive marketing. Several examples can be cited:

The Norwegian government passed a law banning the use of promotional competition in the retail food industry. Large food stores were attracting customers away from smaller stores and from each other through high intensity promotion programs. This raised the cost of doing business and, in the end, raised food prices. Although the ban on promotional competition was at first resisted by the large food chains, its effects are now accepted as beneficial.

The Swedish government is highly concerned with brand proliferation in certain consumer product categories. For example, the Swedish soft drink industry offers many different soft drinks and new ones are introduced all the time. Some members of the government say that excessive resources are tied up in this and other industries to support brand proliferation. They propose product licensing in these industries to permit only brands with significant differences to be introduced.

The Indian government is concerned about the increasing inroads of national brand marketing in basic food categories such as tea, rice, and flour. They see modern branding and packaging as raising the cost of food to the poor and wish to preserve, where possible, bulk selling of basic commodities.

The Philippine government accepts modern branding and packaging but is concerned with the lack of price spread in many product categories. The existence of many brands of soap is acceptable but not the lack of cheap brands for poorer consumers. They call this "false variety" and seek to provide manufacturers with incentives to introduce some less expensive brands along with more expensive brands.

The Mexican government levies a tax on advertising, ostensibly for the purpose of discouraging advertising from becoming excessive.

The concern about falling into an "overmarketing trap" is also expressed in the United States by certain industries just beginning to use marketing. Some hospital administrators see marketing as helpful to the individual hospital today but worry that it will become a fixed expense tomorrow. They anticipate that it will push up hospital costs without corresponding gain, just as trading stamps act as an asset when only one firm offers them and a liability when all firms offer them. They worry that today's bright solution—marketing—will become tomorrow's problem.

Societal Overmarketing

A growing body of criticism charges that American society as a whole exhibits overmarketing. The great interest of Americans in material acquisition is not seen as an accidental cultural trait but rather as a built-in feature of industrial capitalism. Business hires Madison Avenue to stimulate people's desires for goods. Madison Avenue uses the mass media to create materialistic models of the good life. Conspicuous consumption on the part of some creates desires by others. Self-concepts move toward congruency with this version of the good life. Individuals work harder to earn the necessary money. This increases the output and productive capacity of the Industrial State. In turn, the Industrial State makes greater use of Madison Avenue to stimulate desire for the industrial output. Thus, people are seen as a manipulated link in the cycle between production and consumption. Wants come to depend on output. This is what Galbraith calls the "dependence effect." In his words:

> The control or management of demand is, in fact, a vast and rapidly growing industry in itself. It embraces a huge network of communications, a great array of merchandising and selling organizations, nearly the entire advertising industry, numerous ancillary research, training and other related services and much more. In everyday parlance this great machine, and the demanding and varied talents that it employs, are said to be engaged in selling goods. In less ambiguous language it means that it is engaged in the management of those who buy goods.[12]

Vance Packard, another major marketing critic, tries to establish that Americans are unaware of manipulation:

> This book . . . is about the large-scale efforts being made, often with impressive success, to channel our unthinking habits, our purchasing decisions, and our thought processes by the use of insights gleaned from psychiatry and the social sciences. Typically these efforts take place beneath our level of awareness; so that the appeals which move us are often, in a sense, "hidden." The result is that many of us are being influenced and manipulated, far more than we realize, in the patterns of our everyday lives.[13]

The result, according to Herbert Marcuse, is "false" needs:

> "False" (needs) are those which are superimposed upon the individual by particular social interests. Most of the prevailing needs to relax, to have fun, to behave and consume in accordance with the advertise-

ments, to love and hate what others love and hate, belong to this category of false needs.[14]

These critics accuse marketing of getting the public to buy things that it
doesn't need, doesn't want, and often can't afford, all for the sake of keeping
production going and creating profits for the owners of private capital. The
result is high growth of *gross national product* but not necessarily growth of *net
national welfare.* They see high consumption as creating "bads" as well as
"goods"—pollution, environmental destruction, noise, self-centeredness,
cultural anarchy. They feel that too much attention is devoted to getting and
spending at the sacrifice of other values important to society, such as altruism,
sharing, quiet, simplicity, respect for the aged, preservation of the environment, and so on.

Disenchantment with uncontrolled capitalism has expressed itself in recent
years in the emergence of such social movements as consumerism, environmentalism, and anti-industrialism. Government regulation of marketing practices continues to increase over time with the full approval of the public and
the dismay of the business community. The intent behind new marketing constraints is both to make marketing better and to contain it from getting much
larger as a facet of social life. Marketers bring some of this wrath upon themselves by acting as if the goal of economic society is to maximize material consumption rather than to deliver a high quality of life to citizens.

THE FUTURE OF MARKETING

The years 1950-70 represent the golden age of economic growth in which
nations nourished the hope that their citizens could realize ever improving
standards of living. This dream was shattered in the early 1970s with the oil
crises and the growing concern over exhaustible resources. *Limits to Growth*[15]
and other studies argued that key resources were too limited to permit the realization of unlimited material progress for mankind. Unless miraculous technological breakthroughs occurred, it was held that nations would have to
begin to find ways to put the brakes on want creation. Nations would have to
replace the bright ethic of consumption with the pale ethic of conservation.

In the face of mounting costs and risks of uncontrolled economic growth,
we can expect that business and marketing practices will be subject to new
constraints as well as new opportunities. We expect to see the following developments in marketing over the next decade.

Increased Government Regulation of Marketing Practices

Consumer and environmental groups will press hard on legislators to examine and to regulate various marketing practices. Advertising will continue to draw fire, and proposals will be advanced to control its quantity and pass on its quality. Packaging practices will attract increased attention from those concerned with problems of waste and pollution. Product development practices in certain industries beyond pharmaceuticals, automobiles, and toys will be burdened with new regulations in the interest of public health and safety. Pricing and distribution practices will be studied for any evidence of anticompetitive behavior. All of this will necessitate more involvement by company lawyers in decisions covering almost all the elements of the marketing mix.

Financial Accountability

Firms will increasingly apply financial yardsticks to their marketing plans and results. More companies are holding marketing management responsible for profits and not just sales. Some product managers even have to answer for their inventory levels and their receivables in accounting for their performance. A number of companies have established marketing controllership positions occupied by financial executives who are expert in analyzing marketing costs and productivity. The marketing vice-president increasingly must show a financial orientation in his development of marketing strategies and choice of marketing efforts.

Elevated Concepts of the Firm's Mission

The American corporation is undergoing a subtle transformation from strictly private enterprise to quasi-public enterprise. Focus on profit performance is not enough. Some corporations are beginning to take account of their impact on their workers' lives, their immediate communities, their customers' well-being, and the society as a whole. Many corporations are pioneering new roles for the corporation in connection with job enrichment and social responsibility.[16] They are trying to define their business mission in the broadest possible human terms so that all the parties connected with the company see it as a worthwhile organization. A vacuum cleaner company could define its job as manufacturing vacuum cleaners . . . this is the normal level of business vision. A more enlightened vacuum cleaner company would define its role as dirt removal. At the highest level of enlightenment, a vacuum cleaner company would see its business mission as improving the environment. More corporations in the future will attempt to define their mission in human terms rather than product terms. Ten years ago the International Minerals and Chemicals Company did this by defining itself not as a fertilizer company but as a company trying to fight the problem of world hunger. This vision aroused great enthusiasm among the managers, employees, distributors, and customers. Hand-in-hand with creating a human-centered mission will go changes in marketing practices that will reflect a more humanistic approach to customers and their needs. Corporations will become more reluctant to use bait advertising and sharp selling practices that work on the emotions of the consumer and, instead, try to sell the real qualities of the firm and its products.

Consumer Education and Information

Our society fails to spend enough for meaningful consumer education and information. Young people experience a few poorly taught home economics courses in their public education; fewer than two million people subscribe to monthly *Consumer Reports* evaluating commonly purchased products; and most people depend on the slanted product information provided through advertising and personal selling. In comparison, the Scandinavian economies make a greater public investment in consumer education. In Sweden, for example, students take several years of "life" courses in which they learn how to buy such things as clothing, automobiles, and insurance; how to make bank loans; how to repair things; and how to evaluate advertising and sales arguments. Increased pressure for heightened investment in consumer education is appearing in the United States. To the extent this movement is successful, it will lead to a public that is in a much better position to judge value in relation to price. Firms that offer good value in relation to price will benefit; others will face increasing consumer resistance and will be in danger of falling behind.

Marketing's Migration into Nonprofit Industries

Marketing ideas and techniques will show an increasing rate of penetration into the nonprofit sector of the economy. Currently, the health industry and the college industry are very excited about marketing thinking as it bears on their difficult competitive situations. Similarly, many museums, symphonies, and theatrical groups are turning to marketing for both audience development and fundraising.

Increasing Role of Social Marketing

Until now, marketing has not been utilized to any significant extent by government agencies to solve social problems through influencing the public to perform or to desist from certain behaviors. However, this situation is changing. Marketing activities are now being undertaken to help gain support for family planning, mass transit, preventative health behavior, and conservation. We can imagine in the future large scale marketing plans being developed by government marketers to encourage changes in public attitudes and behavior to bring these more into line with social and ecological imperatives.

CONCLUSION

Marketing has come a long way in its short history. It has ripened into a useful discipline in the business and nonbusiness sectors of the economy. It has given precision to concepts of demand and consumer interest. In the new environment, it will undoubtedly undergo further transformations in order to serve both individual need and the public interest. Marketing is not at the end of its life cycle but rather in a transitional stage in which it is about to take on new roles and responsibilities.

NOTES

1. F. H. Elsby, in private correspondence.
2. Robert Bartels, *The History of Marketing Thought*, Second Edition (Columbus, Ohio: Grid, 1976), p. 24.
3. *Ibid.*

4. Peter F. Drucker, *Management: Tasks, Responsibilities, Practices* (New York: Harper & Row, 1973), p. 62.

5. *Ibid.*, pp. 124-25.

6. *Ibid.*, p. 63.

7. William H. Hornby, "Beware the 'Market' Thinkers . . . ," *The Quill* (1976): p. 14 ff. However, see William A. Mindak, "Do Newspaper Publishers Suffer from 'Marketing Myopia'?," *Journalism Quarterly* (Summer 1965).

8. Theodore Levitt, "Marketing Myopia," *Harvard Business Review* (September-October 1975), pp. 26-44, 173-81.

9. Drucker, *Management*, p. 64.

10. Ralph Z. Sorenson II, "U.S. Marketers Can Learn from European Innovators," *Harvard Business Review* (September-October 1972): p. 97.

11. This description is taken verbatim from a letter from a well-known management consultant who prefers anonymity.

12. John Kenneth Galbraith, *The New Industrial State* (Boston: Houghton Mifflin, 1967), p. 200.

13. Vance Packard, *The Hidden Persuaders* (New York: Pocket Books, 1957), p. 1.

14. Herbert Marcuse, *One-Dimensional Man* (Boston: The Beacon Press, 1964), pp. 4-5.

15. Donella H. Meadows *et al., The Limits to Growth* (New York: Signet, 1972).

16. Lee Loevinger, "Social Responsibility in a Democratic Society" in *Business Problems of the Seventies,* ed. Jules Backman (New York: New York University Press, 1973), Chapter 9.

FOUR

The Team Approach to

Strategic Marketing Planning

Arnold Corbin

Professor Emeritus of Marketing
New York University

Before developing the concept of the team approach, we shall first deline-ate some of the underlying forces which underscore the need for market-oriented planning and for a unified planning system. We shall then briefly deal with the transcending importance of getting the involvement and partici-pation of all functions of the business in the planning process, and set forth some fundamental philosophical concepts underlying successful planning. With these as a background, we shall proceed to develop the concept and methodology of the team approach. Finally, the principal advantages and benefits of the team approach will be spelled out.

THE NEED FOR MARKET-ORIENTED PLANNING

There are four main forces at work in the business world today that make it important to plan marketing strategies systematically, so that full advantage of opportunities may be taken, and thereby long-range targets for growth and profit achieved. These four factors are:

1. The increasing size and complexity of business organizations;
2. The sharply stepped-up pace of competition;

3. The increasingly rapid rate of change in both the technological and marketing environments; and
4. The increasing pressure for new products and markets.

Increasing Size and Complexity of Business

Managing a business today is much more complex and difficult than it used to be, and it is likely to become even more so in the future as products, packages, and markets expand and as organizations grow in size. Furthermore, the cost of making a mistake—either of commission or of omission—is going up. The era of "management by intuition," when managers could be successful by simply dealing with each "crisis" as it arose, has been rapidly drawing to a close. A new era of planning and management by objective is at hand.

Greater Competition

Secondly, increasingly intense competition in the future will make it harder to improve—or even to maintain—market position and to protect profits and profit margins. And it is quite likely that this increased competition will come not only from the firms and products which are now in the marketplace, but also from new sources and in new forms. These very real competitive threats to markets, growth, and profits make it essential that managers plan more effective use of marketing and other resources to improve their strategies and develop the weapons that will not only answer these threats, but also insure market leadership in the years ahead.

Change in Technology and Markets

In addition to the increasing size and complexity of operations and the growing severity of competition, there is a third important force which underscores the necessity for a sound marketing planning system as the basis for decisions that will affect the future of a business. This force is change—change in technology and change in markets—change which is now occurring, and which will continue to occur in the future at an accelerating rate. Besides the changes which are directly attributable to the explosion in technological innovations, managers must be particularly aware of and concerned with other kinds of changes which are altering the fundamental character of markets: shifts in the location of customers and consumers; in patterns of consumer taste, usage, buying habits and preferences; in distribution methods and channels; and even in buyer-seller relationships. The impact of consumerism and environmentalism also must be considered.

Adaptation to these changes is probably one of the major challenges that faces marketing managers as they attempt to make the best decisions with respect to the future. Hence, the need to turn to marketing research and planning to keep the business attuned to the changing character and tempo of the marketplace. Success in meeting this challenge will depend upon the ability to conceive and implement creative marketing plans, policies, and programs, not only to stay abreast of rapidly accelerating market changes and technological advances, but also to move ahead of competition and increase market share.

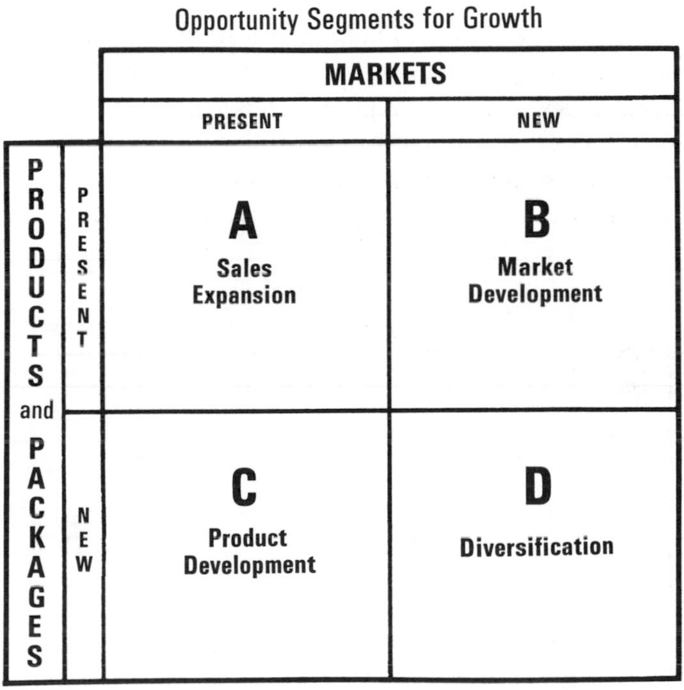

Opportunity Segments for Growth

	MARKETS	
	PRESENT	**NEW**
PRODUCTS and **PACKAGES** — PRESENT	**A** Sales Expansion	**B** Market Development
NEW	**C** Product Development	**D** Diversification

Fig. 4.1   THE PRODUCT-MARKET MATRIX

Pressure for New Products and Markets

The fourth major force which emphasizes the need for systematic planning is the intensifying urgency for new products, new packages, new markets, and even new methods of distribution—a challenge which promises to become even greater in the years ahead as pressures for growth and profit increase, as the marketplace becomes more competitive, and as consumer wants and preferences change in response to advances in technology and new ways of living and thinking.

The new product-new market challenge which faces managers today is graphically demonstrated in Fig. 4.1. Cell A on this chart reflects the sales of the products and packages in the line to present customers and market segments. Cell B represents the opportunity to expand the business by moving with the present product and package mix into new markets. On the other hand, Cell C is based on adding other products and packages to the line but marketing them to the same markets that are now served. Finally, Cell D indicates the opportunity to diversify in terms of new products going into new markets.

A glance at this chart seems to indicate that equal amounts of time, effort, and resources are being devoted to each of the four activities, i.e., sales expansion (A), market development (B), product development (C), and diversification (D).

However, the real world does not always look this way, as may be noted in

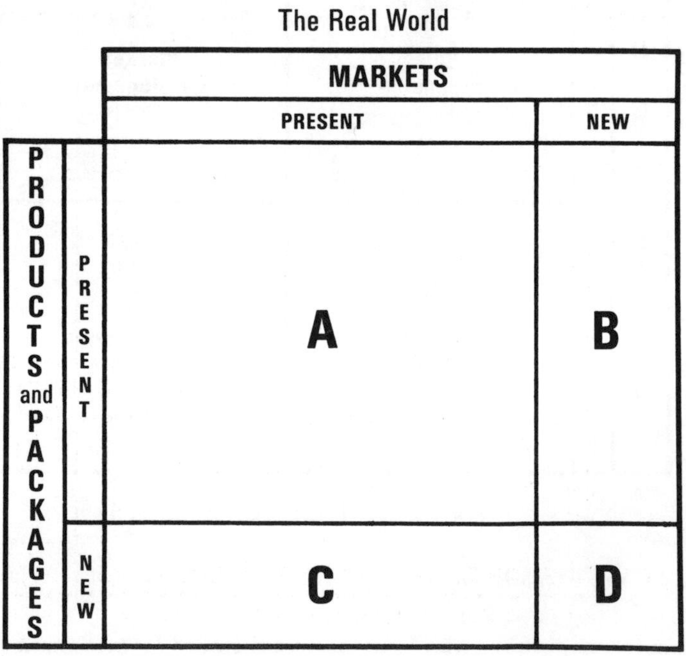

Fig. 4.2   THE PRODUCT-MARKET MATRIX

Fig. 4.2. Unfortunately, there is a tendency for some managers in the business world to concentrate the bulk of energy and resources in segment A, selling present products in present markets. When this occurs, not enough attention can be devoted to the other three segments, B, C, and D. In a sense one might call this "marketing myopia." Not only is such an allocation of time and money myopic; it is indeed risky. Unless the product-market base is expanded by devoting more effort to segments B, C, and D, the chances of achieving growth and profit objectives in the years that lie ahead may be severely diminished. Instead of causing change by moving vigorously into new products, new markets, new ways of distribution, the risk is run of becoming the victim of such changes which may be caused by more forward-looking competitors.[1]

Product Life Cycle

New products and new markets are the life blood of all business. They are the requisites of good health and vigorous growth, and they will be even more important in the future as the so-called "Product Life Cycle" speeds up and becomes even shorter in duration.

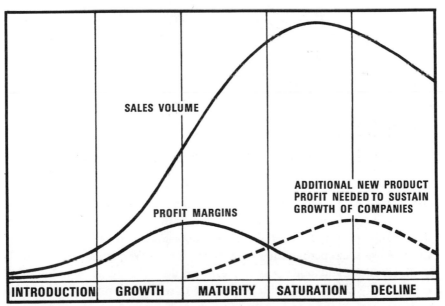

SOURCE: MANAGEMENT RESEARCH DEPARTMENT BOOZ-ALLEN & HAMILTON

Fig. 4.3 THE BASIC LIFE CYCLE OF NEW PRODUCTS

As can be seen on Fig. 4.3, new products, like people, go through a "life cycle" of introduction, growth, maturity, saturation, and decline. It should be noted, however, that the peak in profit margins (in *percentage* terms) is reached long before the peak in sales volume. This means that if a business is to continue to grow profitably, it must constantly seek new or improved products to add to its line or new users and uses for its present products.

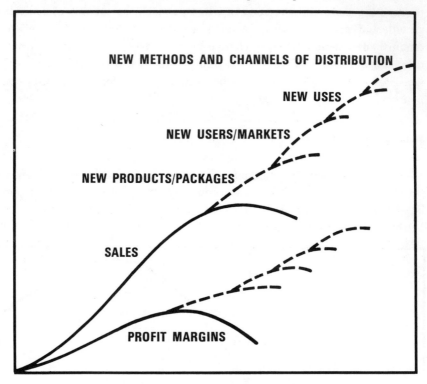

Fig. 4.4   GIVING THE PRODUCT LIFE CYCLE A BOOST

This point is illustrated graphically in Fig. 4.4. As may be readily noted, just "letting nature take its course" is an unaffordable decision. The price of senility is high. In planning the future of a business, one must be constantly alert to the necessity for capitalizing on opportunities to expand markets, to find new users and perhaps new uses for products, new methods and channels of distribution, and other ways to give product life cycles new bursts of vitality. Only in this way will it be possible to realize the full potential of the business, to close the so-called "planning gap," and to reach planned growth and profit objectives.

This will get harder to do in the future as the product life cycle gets shorter and shorter, because of the ever faster pace of technological and market change. In earlier years, it took a relatively small amount of time, effort, and money to develop a product and introduce it to the market. Sales increased over a much longer period of time before they began to decline. Today it takes a great deal more time, effort, and money to develop a product and it is much more difficult, dangerous, and expensive to introduce it to the market. If one is fortunate, sales rise rapidly, but they may also fall off more rapidly. Risk increases as the cycle shortens.

Gap Analysis

Another way to look at this problem of product-market expansion is in terms of *gap analysis*, i.e., its usefulness in helping to close the gap between the so-called "momentum line" and the so-called "potential line." Gap analysis can be applied with equal validity to products, packages, and markets, as well as to businesses. In other words, it is important that management plan ahead to determine the rate of growth in sales and earnings, as well as the return on investment which it desires to achieve during some predetermined future period, within the type or types of business it has predefined as its sphere of operation. Having set these objectives, it can then project what would happen if it relied solely on selling present products in present markets (momentum). It can then determine the size of the "growth gap" that must be filled by new products (or packages) and markets, or other activities, in order that it may reach the goals it has set for growth and profit.

A New Climate

To sum up, one might say that the increasing size and complexity of business organizations, and the sharply stepped-up pace of competition, technological advance, market change, and new product-market development, have combined to create a new climate for managing the business—one that is completely different from that of only a short time ago. This new climate, forcibly and forcefully, emphasizes the need for better decision-making in the future for better planning, direction, and control of operations.

In the current environment of business, the options available are increasing rapidly in number. At the same time, the speed with which one has to anticipate or respond to change is also increasing. To select as effectively as possible among these options and to program the actions that will be most productive in achieving objectives calls for a creative combination of management judgment and a factual basis for effective decision-making. In other words, once "the business we are in" has been clearly defined, an organized system of unified planning and implementation is required to assure that the rifle rather than the shotgun concept is used in deploying funds and efforts against the targets which will produce the best results in terms of growth and profit.

NEED FOR A UNIFIED MARKETING PLANNING SYSTEM

It is quite apparent that marketing is one of the most important functions in the business. This activity, in fact, should provide the spearhead for the formulation, implementation, and control of strategic plans for the total business. Thus, it follows that a systematic approach to marketing planning is essential if strategic plans are to be carried out successfully and both current and future potentials for growth maximized in an environment of constant change and increasingly aggressive, skillful competition. Said in a slightly different way, an integrated marketing planning system is helpful in identifying, in an orderly way, the opportunities available to realize optimum results from existing business and from new products, new packages, new markets, and even new concepts of marketing, which should be capitalized on if the challenge of the future is to be met. Therefore, it is important to aim for a *unified* system of marketing planning—a system in which all components of the business follow substantially identical, or at least very similar, approaches and procedures.

A substantial degree of uniformity in planning processes throughout the organization has many obvious advantages. In the first place—and this is probably one of the principal advantages—a unified system will, to a large extent, reduce the possibility of duplication of work and expense which can certainly occur if, in various component units, systems are devised that differ markedly in format but little in substance. In the second place, the unified marketing planning system is designed so that, to the greatest extent possible, key information or planning data which higher echelons may require for their own purposes can be supplied in the form of copies of schedules which lower echelons have already prepared for their own use. Obviously, for this principle to be effective, uniformity is essential so that those individuals at higher levels who examine and analyze such data can readily understand their nature and meaning, and, when useful to do so, can readily compare them with similar data from other locations or components. A further advantage of a unified marketing system is that it facilitates the interchange of marketing personnel among different organizational units of a company. Based on experience gained in using uniform procedures, key personnel who are transferred from one location or unit to another can become effective in their new post within a much shorter period of time.

BETWEEN MARKETING AND THE OTHER MAJOR FUNCTIONS

Marketing planning, implementation, and control, in order to be effective, require the close cooperation, coordination, and exchange of ideas and information among all the major functional groups involved in the business. These include corporate strategic planning, financial, research and development, production, and legal, as well as marketing. Any planning system must, of course, be a realistic and practical tool. Any successful marketing planning system must be predicated on a clear and continuing relationship between marketing and the other key functions upon which the profitable growth of the company depends. As Mr. J. Fred Bucy, president of Texas Instruments has so aptly put it: "A company has three main functions: create, make, and market. All three must be interwoven in corporate philosophy, organization, and system."[2]

The planning process, once there has been a clear-cut definition of the business the company is in, starts in the market. Inputs from the marketplace arc essential to both marketing planning and strategic corporate or business planning. The central focal point of the process is the marketing plan and its implementation. In the development of an orderly, integrated system, all of the functions or "resource owners" involved have to work in concert. The emphasis which the systems approach to marketing management places on interaction and teamwork in the planning and decision-making process is illustrated by the two-way interlinkage and flow among the functions. The precise nature of this interaction will be developed at a later point when we cover the details of the way the team approach to marketing planning operates.

At this point, only some broad observations about the nature of the inputs involved need be made. Financial people participate at appropriate points in the planning process since it is essential that the financial implications of marketing plans be set out clearly. Such details as *pro forma* contribution-to-profit statements and estimates of return on investment should clearly be included in marketing plans. Furthermore, there should be a close linkage between the financial aspects of marketing plans and the budgeting process.

The development and launching of a new product illustrates the necessity for close interfunctional participation between marketing and R & D in the planning process. It would be meaningless to develop a plan for a new product introduction without considering at the same time all the related decisions that would have to be made with respect to the development and testing of the optimum design or formulation from the consumer point of view, its packaging, its impact on production and distribution facilities, the costs of advertising and marketing the product, its contribution to profit, its trademark and other legal aspects, and so on.

It cannot be emphasized too strongly that total business planning should focus on the marketplace—with customers and consumers—not on the manufacturing plant. There must be agreement among all members of management that the marketplace is the integrative basis for planning throughout the company, with full recognition, nevertheless, for the role of technological innovation in the process.

It logically follows, therefore, that the marketing plan should become the keystone element in the total business plan.[3] This implies that marketing management should assume a leadership role in discovering market opportunities and helping to marshall all company resources to take full advantage of them. In other words, once we have zeroed in on unsatisfied market needs, we can then concentrate our research and other energies on developing products or services which the market will recognize as filling its needs, rather than hoping the market will accept what we have already "invented." Marketing, as the integrative force, should attempt to secure the full involvement and commitment of the other main "resource owners" of the business, namely, the people in R & D, engineering, production, and finance, as well as strategic planning. The best results are obtained when they all work together as a team to develop the marketing plan, which then becomes the basis for the R & D plan, the production plan, and the financial plan. The individual functional plans are then integrated into a master plan for the whole business, which, of course, should be consonant with the preagreed definition of the business the company or other organizational unit is in or desires to be in.

Within Marketing: Among Marketing Subfunctions

The importance of all the major functions in the business working together to get the best results out of the planning process has already been stressed. The same principle applies with equal force within the marketing activities of the business as well.

Unless the planning system is so organized that the maximum degree of involvement and commitment is attained on the part of marketing personnel who are responsible for the various marketing functions, products, and market segments, the risk is run that best possible results may not be achieved. Each activity may conceivably do an excellent job by itself, but this does not necessarily mean that when all the individual plans are put together an optimum situation will result. There is the ever-present danger that too much energy may be concentrated on "doing the thing right" (efficiency) instead of first asking, "Are we doing the right thing?" (effectiveness).

Hence, a well-organized system of marketing planning must make provision for the close coordination of the activities of all marketing personnel. Only in this way will they be able to make proper contributions at the right time to the various marketing plans, as well as to integrate ideas and inputs from the other "resource owners" within the marketing function.

SOME FUNDAMENTAL PHILOSOPHICAL CONCEPTS

A few basic philosophical ideas that underlie effective marketing planning should be emphasized. These thoughts have been distilled from my experience with, and knowledge of, a number of companies which have spent years in developing marketing planning systems that really work.

The objective of a good planning system is the creation of plans that contain really innovative ideas for moving the business ahead. Plans should not be produced for the sake of having plans; otherwise, planning becomes an expensive and wasteful exercise in plan writing. The objective is *not* to produce a mass of papers and forms.

Companies which have developed a good planning system have found that the original plans were massive volumes. In subsequent planning cycles, the size of the plans gradually have shrunk, so that, several years later, the superior plans have been short, concise, and have contained only the essence of creative ideas, strategies, and methods for effective implementation.[4] The planning in these companies is now increasingly concentrated on the relatively few key activities that may make or break the business. The lesson to be learned is not to plan every activity in the business with an equal degree of detail, but to concentrate the heaviest planning energy on the major activities.

As a corollary principle, one must be very careful to avoid regarding the planning process as an exercise in simply filling in numbers on forms. The emphasis should be on substance and not form. In other words, the highest payout comes from creative, innovative ideas in terms of products, or markets, or even new ways of marketing, rather than merely going through the motions of executing the particular forms in a system. Here is where the quality of insight is so important: the ability to analyze various bits and pieces of data which, when integrated with one's knowledge, experience, and intuition, may yield the synergy that can discover and capitalize on real opportunities in the marketplace—opportunities to fill unsatisfied consumer needs profitably.

This is particularly important in the multiproduct, multimarket business of today. For example, since resources are normally scarce and limited, one must be very careful in planning to assure that they are allocated optimumly among the different products in the line and among the various market segments into which they move. Thus, planning decisions with respect to the timing and quantity of resources to be allocated among various products and market segments should be consonant with previously determined objectives and strategies designed to advance the welfare of the business as a whole. The aim, therefore, is to avoid the danger of suboptimization by myopic concentration on each product of each market segment without proper evaluation of the effect on the total operation. In other words, if maximum effectiveness is to be achieved in planning, one must be careful not to miss the "forest" (the business as a whole) for the individual "trees" (the various products, market segments, and other elements of the business).

Planning Should Not Be Separated from Running the Business

A contributing factor to the skepticism which some companies have about the value of planning is the failure to integrate the *planning* of the business with the *running* of the business. Too much marketing planning is carried on as a parallel activity with running the business, rather than the *basis* for it. In other words, planning is too often done for planning's sake alone, and not as the strategic and tactical blueprint for operating the business.

For a marketing planning system to be effective it is essential that the people who run the business should also be responsible for planning the business. To divorce the two activities does not generally produce the best results. The reason for this is that plans should be used as blueprints for actually operating a business and making the key decisions. Then these results become valid inputs for the next planning cycle—or even revisions of the current plan, if necessary—before the planning period has been completed. Only in this way can planning be made realistic.

This is not to say that the executives who manage various marketing activities should not be given help in their planning by staff people who are spe-

cialists in particular phases of planning and information acquisition. However, the basic responsibility for developing and implementing plans should
remain with the key managers in the business.

In a nutshell, the point being emphasized is that the marketing manager
and each of the other managers under him in the marketing operations of the
business should not only make their plans but also implement them, and
evaluate the results as the basis for the next cycle of planning.

The Need for Top Management Support and Commitment

Achieving success in planning is a difficult task at the very least. It should
therefore be given every possible help and guidance from top management.
This principle applies not only to the basic philosophical attitudes of top executives, but also to the concomitant obligations they must assume in order
for the planning system to work properly.

Success in marketing planning is contingent on securing the full support,
involvement, and commitment of top management. This means making it
clear to all managers in the business that top management does believe in
planning, that it will implement an organized system for accomplishing planning, that the people involved will be given the time to get the planning done,
and that it will provide specific guidelines to appropriate planning echelons.

The Need for the "Team Approach"

The necessity for a close working relationship among the major functions
of the business, and among the principal functions and activities of the
marketing part of the business, has already been indicated. In order to accomplish this successfully both *involvement* and *commitment* are needed. These are
best achieved when the managers of the business, at the different echelons,
plan and operate together as a team. This "team approach" to planning will
now be expanded and developed more fully.

THE TEAM APPROACH

Basic Concept

Based upon many years of experience in helping a number of major companies in both the industrial and consumer fields set up result-oriented sys-

tems of planning, I am firmly convinced that the most effective planning occurs when all the principal resource owners and functional managers do the planning, as well as the running of a business, or a marketing operation, or the developing of a project, *as a team*. The key concepts that underwrite successful planning and implementation are *involvement* and *commitment*. One sure way to condemn a plan and the planning process to failure is to delegate the planning job to a planner who locks himself in his office and designs the plan in splendid isolation, leaving it up to others to implement.

The key premise here is that for *planning* to be effective, it should be done by the same people who are responsible for *running* the business or *developing* the project. Obviously then, the reverse proposition holds equally true, that is, the *operating* will be effective because the planning is done by the same people who operate.

Thus, instead of "planning" and "operating" running along parallel tracks that never meet, they are fully integrated at all times. There isn't one group of "planners" and another group of "operators." They are one and the same. Planning is not something one man does and then turns over to another for execution.

Viewed this way, planning and implementation are not discrete steps to be performed by different people according to a precisely preordained timetable. Rather, the whole cycle must be regarded as one of continuous action and feedback so that planning and implementation interlock dynamically, each inducing substantive change, correction and improvement in the other, without excessive preoccupation with the highly artificial "man-made" constraint called the calendar.

I do not subscribe to the following version (or perhaps perversion) of the old cliché: "Those who can, do; those who can't, plan!"

Because the team approach is predicated on the team members wearing two "hats" (that is, they do both the planning and the operating), it goes far to overcome the problem of lack of integration between the planning and the running of the business.

Another important point: the principle that planning should be a team activity applies equally at *all* echelons in the organization, although the composition of the team obviously changes as one moves down through the echelons. Thus, at the top would be the members of the *business* team (top management functional heads). The next level would be the members of the *functional* teams, led by the manager of the function and comprising the managers of the subfunctions. The applicability of the team approach within each echelon will be treated within the sections which follow.

Applicability to Interfunctional Business Planning

Members of the interfunctional business planning team might include the general manager, as well as representatives from marketing, R & D, production, finance, and any other functions which could make a significant contribution to the success of the particular planning effort.[5] In this manner, marketing planning becomes an integral and vital part of *total business planning,* as it rightfully should be.

This integration may be accomplished by use of the team approach. For example, the marketing manager, along with the other key functional managers, participates in the total business planning process: he provides important inputs and he makes solid commitments to his teammates. As a result, the business plans that emerge are realistically market oriented.

By this involvement in the over-all planning effort, the marketing manager is then in a much better position to guide his own marketing associates as he and they proceed to develop and build the basic strategic marketing plan together as well as the subplans for products, markets, and functions.

Some examples of the team approach that demonstrate the opportunity for cooperation among major functions of the business may be worth citing at this point.

The team approach not only encourages effective cross-functional integration at the interface between *marketing* and *R & D,* but also helps underwrite a strong *market orientation.* Since the marketing manager becomes a full and equal partner in the business of planning, he can take the leadership in focusing the energies of his peers on finding market opportunities, and marshalling all the resources they represent (especially technology), to take full advantage of them. Full expression of the customer point of view is thus insured at a stage early enough in the planning cycle to influence the thinking of the team members representing the technological side of the business. Conversely, they, as equal partners in planning, can temper the marketing view with important, pertinent technological considerations. In the process, the team can hopefully hammer out an optimum, innovative, synergistic approach that builds on both marketing and technology.

The product planning and development process offers a fine proving ground for the application of this interfunctional approach at the interface between *marketing* and *R & D.* In those companies which subscribe to this concept, the idea of continuing interaction and communication between the "product" side and the "market" side as the development process evolves is paramount.

The team approach can also do much to forge a strong bond of reciprocal interdependence between the *marketing* and *financial* functions in a company. The marketing concept clearly assigns a profit responsibility to the marketing organization. Since management is primarily interested in results, marketing executives must be managers of money as well as marketers of goods and services. In order to implement the concept effectively, therefore, marketing people require a steady flow of profit-oriented information from financial people to help them make sound planning and control decisions and understand the financial implications of their decisions. Even more importantly, they need professional guidance in the application of the newest financial and accounting concepts and techniques, such as break-even analysis, contribution, payback period, return on investment, discounted cash flow (DCF), direct costing versus absorption costing, and so on. Concepts such as these should be in the daily lexicon of marketing people—not merely relegated to the lexicon, but used, too. How will this come to pass if we do not organize and operate to insure that such knowledge is imparted to marketers by financially sophisticated people?

Conversely, financial people, traditionally more manufacturing oriented than marketing oriented, need to know much more about the marketing concept and about the financial information and decision-making needs of the revenue producers (the marketing people) and how marketing decisions affect the financial results of operations, i.e., receivables, inventory, profit, and so on. The problem is essentially one of inducing a free two-way flow of communication between the marketing and control functions.

Marketing Controller

I would, therefore, advocate what seems to me to be a clear-cut organizational implication of this need for a closer liaison—the concept of a marketing controller—who could be a member of the controller's staff (or, for that matter, anyone well trained in financial accounting and control work), physically located in the marketing department and with line responsibility to marketing management but with a close working relationship with the controller. Preferably, he or she should have had some practical sales and marketing experience as well. In effect, the "marketing controller" is an "in-house accountant" in the marketing department.[6]

Among the several companies that have already adopted this pioneering organizational concept,[7] with substantial success, the incumbent is sometimes called "profit manager," or "marketing cost consultant," or "marketing controller," but the objective is the same. The aim is to insure profit maximization for the total company by helping marketing managers take full advantage of the best and newest financial and accounting techniques to improve their decisions, to plan and control their operations, and to insure maximum return on investment for the company as a whole.

Applicability to Intrafunctional Marketing Planning

While I have referred at various points to "the marketing plan," it should be realized that the reference is not necessarily to any single plan, but actually to a series of plans which, when integrated, do constitute the over-all marketing plan. Thus, there may be a basic strategic or "master" plan, a product or brand plan, a market plan by segment, and also individual functional plans, such as for advertising, sales promotion, sales and so on.

The applicability of the team approach in the development of these various types of marketing plans will be treated with reference, first, to the basic strategic marketing plan, and second, to the various subplans.

Strategic Marketing Plan

It should be emphasized that the keystone element in the system of marketing plans is the basic strategic plan. It sets out the major objectives and strategies for marketing for the particular period being planned. In developing this master plan for marketing, inputs should, of course, flow from the basic strategic plan for the business, particularly in terms of the markets and products that will provide the basis for closing the gap between the so-called "Momentum Line" and the "Plan Line." In other words, basic decisions taken with respect to the directions in which the entire business will be moving, particularly in terms of over-all objectives and strategies, should provide pertinent guidelines to those charged with the preparation of the basic marketing plan. Furthermore, information developed in the process of preparing the strategic business plan, such as the environmental analysis, should also provide valuable inputs to the basic marketing plan.

It is clear, therefore, that the master marketing plan should receive valuable inputs from, and be consonant with, the strategic business plan. The converse should also be true. Marketing personnel can and should make useful inputs to the strategic planning process, as members of the total business team. In principle, for example, the marketing manager, with the other key managers (finance, manufacturing, R & D, and so on) should participate in the total strategic business planning process. His experience and knowledge put him in a position to provide important inputs and make achievable commitments to his teammates. As a result, the strategic plans that emerge should be realistically market oriented. Furthermore, by his involvement in the overall planning efforts, he is then obviously in a much better position to guide his own marketing associates as he and they develop and build the basic strategic marketing plan together.

In developing the strategic marketing plan, the marketing manager acts as the team captain or "prime mover," while the team members might typically include product managers or product planners and the managers of sales, advertising, sales promotion, and marketing research.

Other Marketing Plans

It is vitally important that the various types of marketing subplans closely interlock and be consistent with one another and with the strategic marketing plan so that the best use is made of time, effort, resources, and money in the running of the business. For example, in an organization which operates with product managers, each product manager in generating his *product* plan may find it useful to enlist the cooperation of the key functional managers in the marketing organization (i.e., advertising, sales promotion, marketing research, and so on) as team members who participate with him in the deliberations, contribute information and ideas, and make commitments to ensure the development of the final product plan. Since these *functional* managers participate in building all the product plans, they are then in a position to develop realistic plans for their own functions by integrating the commitments in the individual product plans. Thus, the advertising plan becomes a unified, coordinated summation of the advertising components of all the individual product plans.

Flexibility in terms of interchangeability of roles is the key requirement. Sometimes, it may be helpful to set up special task forces, or teams, with a captain or "project leader" in charge, in order to accomplish the planning for specific objectives or projects.

The use of the team approach in developing the various types of marketing subplans helps to minimize the danger of suboptimizing, or causing disruptions, due to the plans being out of synchronization in either timing or resource deployment. It helps insure that the subplans will be integrated into a master plan which makes the best sense, considering the welfare of the operation as a whole. Furthermore, it is far better to get all the inconsistencies and "pulls" on resources straightened out in the *planning* stage, rather than letting them happen in the *action* stage. This is not only wiser; it also is less risky and less costly.

The team approach possesses another virtue: it capitalizes on the fact that functional managers may be experienced businessmen as well as specialists in their own fields. They may, therefore, have valuable ideas to contribute that go far beyond their particular functional interests. When they actively participate as members of a planning team in looking for new opportunities in the marketplace and deciding on the broad objectives and strategies to capitalize on them, they put on their businessmen's "hats." Then, when each goes back to prepare his own subplan for sales or for advertising for example, he puts on his sales manager's "hat," or his advertising manager's "hat." Having had a voice in making the key decisions of the master plan, he will come up with a far better subplan than if he had not been so consulted, but had simply been told to make it.

The same principle of duality (wearing two hats) applies with equal force and validity to the marketing research function. The marketing *research* manager should be a regular, fully accredited member of the marketing team. This implies that he should be considered not only as a *research specialist* who can make useful inputs to the information base for planning, but also as a *marketing generalist* who can contribute to the decision making of the marketing team in formulating objectives, strategies, and action programs with respect to products and markets, within the framework of overall corporate goals and objectives.

Such recognition of the marketing research man as a fully equal member of the marketing team, along with his peers in the other marketing functions, will go far to alleviate his principal source of frustration, i.e., not being thought of as a full member of the team.[8]

Far more effective research planning will result if the research manager is regarded as a marketing man as well as a researcher. (This, of course, implies that he should possess the necessary credentials and competence to be so regarded.) If he is accorded this status and does participate in the running and the decision making of the marketing operation, he can gain a truly first-hand appreciation of what is going on in the marketplace, with customers and their marketing people, with customers' customers, and so on down the line. Operating at these grass-roots levels, he will be stimulated to generate his own research projects to meet the needs of the operation as he detects them, based upon his own first-hand evidence, instead of waiting solely for second-hand requests from others. His role in initiating research thus changes from a *passive* one to an *active* one. He thereby gains a greater insight into research needs and opportunities and can plan and program research activities with greater realism and effectiveness on a longer-range time scale and within a broader frame of reference.[9]

SOME IMPLEMENTATIONAL GUIDELINES

Set Up a Plan for Planning

If team planning is to be effective, the process must be organized, systematic, and continuous. In other words, one must plan one's planning. It cannot be done on a one-time, hit-or-miss basis, "wedged in" when people are not doing "more important" things. One must be dedicated to the proposition that *team planning* is just as important as *team operating*. The team members must be given adequate time to plan together on a regular, predetermined schedule, as well as to put their team-designed plan into operation and to revise it, if necessary, as feedback controls indicate variances are occurring.

The *modus operandi* of team planning is a series of team sessions, one at each of the principal stages in the evolution of the particular type of plan. Although the purpose of each meeting will obviously vary, the motivating philosophy is to secure *commitment,* based upon a deep sense of *involvement* and a healthy interchange of points of view, among the key people who can make or break a particular project or business. Team sessions as a matter of fact are not concluded until divergent views are reconciled and a consensus emerges to which all team members are committed.

Since one is increasingly operating with scarce resources, especially managerial talent, those operations which have been most successful in planning have found that it makes good sense to designate someone who will be responsible for scheduling the use of these resources optimally in the planning process. This person would, in effect, help design the master plan for *planning,* which would include the scheduling of team sessions to avoid duplication and conflicts, as well as overlapping requests for common resources. In essence, his job would *not* be *to do* any planning *but to see to it that all the planning gets done* more efficiently.

Synthesize "Top-Down" and "Bottom-Up"

A skillful blending of "top-down" strategic guidelines and "bottom-up" grass roots inputs is essential to achieve the best results from the planning effort. Either alone is not sufficient. Strategic conceptions may sometimes have to be tempered to meet the hard realities of the marketplace. Conversely, empirical inputs from the grass roots should normally be evaluated in the light of a sound strategic frame of reference.

Develop a Model Planning Cycle

As an aid to facilitate and implement the team approach to planning, it might be well to construct a model planning cycle in matrix form, as illustrated in Table 4.1.

Down the left-hand side of the table are listed the steps in the planning process, in appropriate chronological order. Across the top of the table six column heads appear, one for each of the various types of marketing plans, i.e., master (strategic), product, market, advertising, sales promotion, and sales-distribution. When the vertical column lines separating types of plans intersect the horizontal lines between the planning steps, cells are created in which may be entered the personnel, by position title, who would logically participate in each step, by type of plan. Also, within each appropriate cell, a code mark might be used to designate the individual who would act as the "prime mover," in the sense that he would assume the responsibility for seeing that proper actions are taken for implementing the particular step concerned. In steps where the team approach is applicable, that individual would operate in the role of team captain.

It will be noted, in Table 4.1 that only Step 1 is spelled out. This was done in the interest of brevity and convenience. The complete listing of the steps in the planning process is as follows:

1. Prepare and disseminate guidelines for planning; provide statement of basic objectives and strategies. (Responsibility of the echelon(s) above each of the levels developing the actual plans themselves).
2. Obtain information and make inputs to INFORMATION BASE/ SITUATION REVIEW. State assumptions where data are incomplete or not available. Audit capabilities, strengths, weaknesses, "faults," "threats," opportunities.
3. Prepare INFORMATION BASE/SITUATION REVIEW.
4. Identify OPPORTUNITIES to be exploited and weaknesses to be overcome.
5. Set OBJECTIVES of the plan.
6. Develop alternative STRATEGIES to achieve objectives.
7. Select optimum STRATEGY.

Table 4.1

THE MARKETING PLANNING CYCLE

Steps in the Planning Process—Participating Personnel by Type of Plan

STEPS IN PLANNING PROCESS	PARTICIPATING PERSONNEL BY TYPE OF PLAN					
	Master (strategic) A	Product B	Market C	Advertising D	Sales Promotion E	Sales/ Distribution F
1. Prepare and disseminate guidelines for planning; provide statement of basic objectives and strategies. (Responsibility of the echelon(s) above each of the levels developing the actual plans themselves)	Division or Operation Manager, based upon guidance and concurrence of higher echelon(s)	Marketing Manager based upon guidance and concurrence of Division or Operation Manager and higher echelon(s)	Same as B	Same as B	Same as B	Same as B
2.						
.						
.						
.						
17.						

8. Identify resource groups necessary for implementation of this strategy.
9. Review, recommend modifications, and approve plan (objectives and strategies).
10. Prepare ACTION PROGRAMS (TACTICS): subplans for each participating resource, including subobjectives, substrategies, action schedules, and time tables (WHO is to do WHAT by WHEN); key tasks, people responsible, deadline dates, dollar and manpower effort required; include IMPLEMENTATION, CONTROL, AND REVIEW procedures.
11. Analyze and modify all subplans; make harmonizing adjustments to arrive at optimum plan.
12. Prepare relevant financial analyses, including *pro forma* contribution statements, return on investment, etc.
13. Prepare "final" total plan, integrating modified subplans, action schedules, and financial analyses.
14. Review, modify, and approve "final" plan.
15. Put plan into operation.
16. Review performance against plan; analyze variances. Take corrective action.
17. Make appropriate modifications and revisions in plan.

It may also be noted, in Table 4.1 that the cells designating participating personnel for steps 2 through 17, by type of plan, are not filled in. The reason is not merely to simplify the table. In this case, the details were omitted because the tremendous variation in organizational structure and position titles makes it impractical to design a universally applicable set of participating personnel by type of plan, for each planning step, to fill in each cell.

However, certain general guidelines and observations are offered which may be of value in implementing the concept.

Step 1 calls for each echelon above the one doing the actual planning to provide the latter with a statement of basic objectives and strategies to be used as a frame of reference. This is an extremely important "first step" to insure that the planners themselves are given appropriate guidelines within which to do their planning. The objective is to prevent wasted time and effort in the generation of plans which, while well designed, may not be consistent with the basic aims of the next higher echelon of the business. The risk lies in the possibility of concentrating on "doing the thing right" (i.e. developing a plan), rather than "doing the right thing" (doing planning that is consonant with predetermined overall objectives and strategies). In other words, one must be careful to avoid "planning myopia." The "macro" guidelines from the echelon above are essential to assure that the "micro" plans that emerge make sense in terms of the frame of reference of the people who will be reviewing and approving the plans.

Step 2 should involve all the relevant resource owners of functional personnel whose factual contributions and analytical judgments are required for each type of plan.

Step 3 requires the synthesis of all the data, assumptions, and other assessments produced in Step 2. It is an integrating step best delegated to one person; in many cases, the task is performed by the marketing research manager, or his designee.

Steps 4 through 8 should normally be treated as a single step in constructing the cell for each type of plan. The basic reason for grouping these five closely related steps is that the participating personnel within any one type of plan should usually be the same for all five of these steps.

An important corollary reason is that these five steps are the ones that should be taken at a single session of the respective teams responsible for particular activities of the business. After the individual members of a planning and operating team have done their homework as individuals (studied their respective information base/situation reviews), they assemble as a team for the next series of major steps in the planning process. Thus, at this meeting, they identify and agree on the key opportunities and problems, set objectives, develop alternative strategies, select the optimum strategy, and finally identify the resource groups necessary to implement this strategy. In other words, they move through steps 4 through 8 in this team planning session.

Certain other points may be worth noting in connection with the accomplishment of these five steps as a unit in the planning process. As indicated earlier, it is felt that the best plans emerge when they are based upon both "bottom-up" and "top-down" participation. Thus, in the sales/distribution plan, designated representatives from the field sales force could be considered an integral part of the planning team. Similarly, the advertising agency could play a contributive role at this stage in the development of advertising plans. By participating in these types of decisions, it should later be able to generate more meaningful and more effective advertising plans and programs.

Step 9 is a critical step which calls for review and approval of what has been accomplished up to this point in the team planning process. Thus, the opportunities, objectives, and strategies set out in the master marketing plan would be checked by the general manager. Similarly, these same elements in the other five types of plans would undergo evaluation by the marketing manager.

There seems to be much wisdom in providing an opportunity for the echelon above to offer its comments and make any additional inputs, including suggested modifications, at this stage. It is certainly far better to get the thinking and opinion of the next echelon(s) upward with respect to opportunities, objectives, and strategies at this point, rather than working out the entire plan, including action programs and subplans, and then submitting it for review and approval. By this method, any suggested revisions in the basic fundamentals of a plan can be incorporated before the details are spelled out. While this step undoubtedly requires some additional time, it offers the offsetting advantage of insuring that the effort devoted to subsequent steps will have a higher payout in the sense that it will be focused on the correct things. In other words, providing this intermediate review and approval step increases the probabilities that the final plan will be "on target." Furthermore, it will simplify the work to be done in Step 14, i.e., review and approval of the final plan. This is because such evaluation will be essentially confined to the actions taken in Steps 10 through 13 covering the detailed implementation of the previously approved objectives and strategies in terms of tactical action programs and subplans.

Steps 10 and 11 should be closely integrated. They are team activities and are accomplished by the same teams as those involved in Steps 4 through 8. This is indeed quite logical under the team approach. After having originally met in a team session to accomplish Steps 4 through 8, the team members then proceed to develop the action programs for the necessary subplans and other details of tactical implementation, including control and review procedures (Step 10). Once these subplans have been prepared, the teams work out the adjustments necessary to arrive at the optimum arrangement (Step 11).

Thus, in essence, Steps 10 and 11 represent the next stage in team planning effort, after the initial results (Steps 4 through 8) have been approved by the next higher echelon(s) (Step 9).

Step 12 calls for some close interfunctional cooperation between marketing and financial personnel in working out the financial implications of the proposed marketing plans. Such joint efforts are necessary also to be sure that the financial data appearing in marketing plans tie in with those appearing in budgets.

Step 13 is an assembly function, and responsibility for it should be with the prime movers for each type of plan.

Step 14 is performed by the respective next higher echelons.

Steps 15, 16, and 17 are characterized by identity of responsibility for performance, i.e., all three are accomplished by the prime mover for each type of plan.

In this section, a generalized "model" of an "ideal" marketing planning cycle has been presented as a basic frame of reference. It should be regarded as a statement of normative principles for integrating, in an optimum manner, the steps in the planning process with the personnel participating in each step, by type of plan. It is hoped that it will prove to be a helpful guide which is flexible enough to be adapted to suit the actual circumstances and requirements of particular organizations.

Advantages and Benefits

The team approach offers a significant array of constructive advantages and synergistic "plusses" to the organization which adopts it and implements it effectively. Among these are:

1. It "pools" the best brainpower in the company and concentrates it on how to plan and run the business better. Nobody has a monopoly on brains.
2. By involving functional heads actively in the planning process right from the beginning, by giving them the opportunity to contribute their ideas to the broad major decisions on opportunities, objectives, and strategies, they develop a strong sense of mutual commitment when it comes to their own efforts as functional specialists. They accept a deep personal responsibility for the successful implementation of their particular subplan. They're not going to be the ones who let their teammates down. There is little risk of an "N.I.H." ("not invented here") reaction, a peculiar "disease" characterized by such symptoms as inertia, apathy, and reluctance that often strikes when people are directed to do something without having been given the prior opportunity to express their ideas on the matter.
3. The consultations among the various functional managers, marketing and nonmarketing, increase the chances of them all being "pointed in the same direction."
4. As a corollary advantage, participation in the team planning effort lessens the tendency for some functional managers to regard their own spheres of operation as "islands"—that is, as being somewhat separate and apart from the other functions.
5. Because planning is now a team affair, based upon mutual respect and understanding, the last step in the planning process, namely, fitting the individual functional subplans into the over-all master plan, becomes a much easier task. It is accomplished by the team working together to

harmonize inconsistencies and overcommitment of resources in the interests of developing the best possible total plan from the point of view of the business as a whole.

6. Finally, nothing succeeds like success. Once team planning gets started and begins to generate plans that achieve good results and that work well in action, a strong sense of purpose—an *esprit de corps*—develops and grows among people in the organization because they know where they are going and how they are going to get there. They are proud to be working with a company that is "with it!"

A Final Thought on the Team Approach

To epitomize and summarize my theme, I have chosen the immortal words of John Donne (English poet, 1572-1631), slightly amended to fit into context:

> "No man(ager) is an island entire
> of itself; every man(ager) is a piece
> of the continent, a part of the main."

The team approach, so conceived and so dedicated, will long endure.

NOTES

1. This imbalance in resource allocation may also result in less-than-optimal linking of long-term and short-term strategy. This is the conclusion of Paul V. Allemang, Officer of the Board, The Mead Corporation. It is to be found in his presentation entitled "Linking Long-Term and Short-Term Strategy," appearing in *Marketing Strategies: A Symposium*, ed. Earl L. Bailey (New York: The Conference Board, 1974), p. 68.

2. J. Fred Bucy, "Marketing in a Goal-Oriented Organization," Chapter 7.

3. This viewpoint is corroborated by David S. Hopkins, Senior Research Associate, The Conference Board. in his words: "Marketing elements of product plans are

more clearly a means to attain business goals. Marketing strategies are folded into business strategies. And even when a product plan is prepared within the marketing department, it may nowadays be described, quite properly, as a business plan." See "New Emphases in Marketing Strategies for an Established Product Line," an address delivered at the Joint Marketing Conference of the Connecticut Chapter of the American Marketing Association and the School of Business Administration of the University of Connecticut, March 11, 1976, pp. 14-15. William F. Christopher, of Hooker Chemical Corporation, goes even further. In his opinion, " . . . the long-range marketing plan and the long-range business plan must be one and the same" in "Marketing Planning That Gets Things Done," *Harvard Business Review* (September-October 1970): p. 64.

4. This trend toward shorter plans is corroborated in a report based on a survey of current planning practices in 162 U.S. and Canadian firms that engage in formal marketing planning and routinely commit their plans to writing. See David S. Hopkins, *The Short-Term Marketing Plan* (New York: The Conference Board, 1972), p. 7.

5. Allemang, *Marketing Strategies,* p. 69, stresses the importance of including the general manager on the interfunctional team. In his words: "Because the general manager's perspectives are terribly important, he has a key role in creating a vital aspect of the linking operation—something I call 'viewpoint mix'!"

6. I first advocated the concept of a marketing controller some ten years ago during the course of a one-day conference I did in London for the British Institute of Management. The idea was expressed in written form in Arnold Corbin and Claire Corbin, *Implementing the Marketing Concept,* First Edition (London: British Institute of Management, 1966), Chapter 8, p. 33, and Revised Edition, (London: British Institute of Management, 1973), Chapter 9, p. 33.

7. DuPont, General Foods, Johnson & Johnson, TWA, and American Cyanamid are among those that have appointed marketing controllers with a financial background. *Business Week,* 28 July 1975, p. 42.

8. Arnold Corbin and Sol Dutka, "Planning Research Strategy," in *Handbook of Marketing Research,* ed. Robert Ferber (New York: McGraw-Hill, 1974), p. 2-47.

9. *Ibid.*

FIVE

Research and the Development

of Marketing Strategy

Gerald J. Glasser

Professor of Business Statistics and Chairman, Marketing Area
New York University

Marketing decisions and marketing strategy are increasingly being based on data provided by research. However, there are many conceptual issues involved in the practice of applying research in marketing, some of which may be briefly summarized as follows:

1. What are the limits of marketing research in terms of quantification, objectivity, and quality?
2. What is the precise role of research in decision-making processes in marketing?
3. On balance, what contribution does market research make to society as a whole? And are there offsetting factors to this contribution?
4. Why are marketing experiments not used more frequently as a tool in research?
5. Does 2 + 2 = 4 in marketing research?

These are rather heavy questions. It is useful, therefore, to begin the discussion with a more basic and perhaps simpler question: "What is market research?" This question is not raised with any hope of answering it definitively but rather to provide a basis for addressing the other questions.

WHAT IS MARKET RESEARCH?

Dictionaries define research in terms that tend to glorify it. Webster's calls it, among other things, "Studious inquiry; usually critical and exhaustive investigation or experimentation. . . . " The World Book Dictionary defines it as "a careful hunting for facts or truth about a subject." The American Heritage Dictionary says it is "scholarly."

So, it seems very clear that we are talking about a good and useful activity—especially as it applies to marketing. A widely held opinion in the field of marketing, at least among academicians, is that market research is marketing's primary cloak of respectability: the ingredient that gives it whatever scientific flavor it has and makes it more astronomy than astrology.

The apparent importance of research in marketing is attested to by its significant continuing growth.

> According to Small and Rosenberg: The acceptance of marketing research as an ongoing corporate function seems well established. A recent update of an American Marketing Association survey . . . indicates the following trends as underlying evidence:
> A steady growth in the number of marketing research departments . . . ;
> An acceleration in the establishment of new marketing research departments in industrial products companies . . . ;
> An upward shift in the corporate reporting structure: approximately 40% of marketing research directors were found to be directly accountable to top management.[1]

Although marketing research is a rapidly expanding field, to some degree—perhaps to a large degree—its growth is more apparent than real. In some cases, the functions of a new department merely border on research and center more on sales promotion or customer relations or some other managerial function. The research director of many of these departments may have little or no technical training in research methodology and virtually no experience in the practice of research. On-the-job training, in my judgment, is not the best way to learn research. Colleges and universities, it seems, still have their work cut out for them in providing market research capability. In brief, the growing demand for research in marketing is a mixed blessing because in many respects it has outraced the supply of research talent.

A DEFINITION OF MARKETING RESEARCH

The official standard definition of marketing research is "the systematic gathering, recording, and analyzing of data about problems relating to the marketing of goods and services."[2]

This attempt at a broad, brief definition has several implications, in terms of exclusions as well as inclusions. These are worth reflecting on, not to criticize the definition nor to improve it, but to better understand what market research is and what it is not.

First of all, what are the problems relating to the marketing of goods and services? A partial listing would relate to such areas of business activity as channels of distribution, pricing, promotional activities, sales force management, nonprice competitive tactics, consumer policy, new product research and development, and advertising. Research, in some sense, can apply and has been applied to any and all phases of marketing.

In a broad sense all market research relates to study of the market. As Boyd and Westfall state:

> The objective of any firm must be rooted in the market place. Unless the firm can satisfy the basic wants and needs of a certain part of the market and do so at a profit, a firm cannot survive. Marketing researchers can play an important role in helping management to think of the firm's objectives in terms of consumer satisfactions in contrast to the more traditional view of products being produced. Management finds it advantageous to think in terms of the *functions* which the product performs instead of in terms of the product *per se.*[3]

Put even more simply, it has been said that the marketing concept is producing what you can sell rather than selling what you can produce. Market research deals with determining what you can sell. Thus, much market research focuses directly on the market with studies of demand to set marketing objectives and strategy to attain those objectives. Such studies may deal with mundane but important questions of consumer purchase patterns—for one's own product and for competing products as well.

Such studies may also deal with the issue of market segmentation. Can the market for a product be defined in terms that set it apart from the general population? Can this market be divided into segments by criteria, measurable by research, such that the segments are susceptible to different marketing strategies? One of the lively debates in market research circles essentially deals with this question. As a recent article by Assael and Roscoe points out:

> Market segmentation has been accepted as a strategic marketing tool to define markets and thereby allocate resources. The concept as originally defined by Wendell Smith requires an "adjustment of product and marketing effort to (differences in) consumer or user requirements." Marketers frequently cite segmentation studies for this purpose, and the term has become something of a buzzword in the literature. A debate has developed between research practitioners as to whether markets can be segmented in a valid and reliable manner. However, a growing number of researchers feel that such studies characteristically fail to account for the important causal variables in purchasing behavior.[4]

Like so many debates, the one on market segmentation offers good and valid points on both sides. It is safe to say that one should neither blindly accept nor blindly reject the segmentation concept.

A good deal of market research is also designed to assess methods of reaching or serving markets. This is illustrated by research to assess the efficiency of individual channels of distribution, by research on sales force functions to allocate sales effort and appropriately reward it, and by research on the effectiveness of advertising.

These comments should suffice to put us in mind of some of the kinds of marketing problems that are relevant in our discussion. Research often has been used to help clarify such problems, and thereby to help solve them. The term *marketing strategy* is used here to mean a plan for action on a marketing problem.

Some less enthusiastic comments on the applications of marketing research should be interjected at this point to keep its role in marketing in perspective. Often marketing research studies are launched with broad, global, and sometimes vague objectives: to assess the overall advertising effectiveness of a campaign, to determine if there is a market for a new product or service, to evaluate present quantity-pricing policy, and so forth.

There is often a tendency to expect too much from research. There are limits to the questions that research can answer, and hence to the problems that research can help solve. Research works best in connection with well-defined, well-structured problems. Failure to recognize the limits of research causes disappointment and disillusionment, and depreciates the worth of research for the problems about which it can make a contribution.

There are, in fact, a number of circumstances in which research should not be used. Lee Adler has nicely capsulized many of the conditions under which this is true, by enumerating situations in which market research should not be conducted.[5] His list includes such factors as:

1. When the cost of the research would exceed its value,
2. When there is an insufficient budget to do a technically adequate job,
3. When research findings would not be actionable,
4. When the problem is not clear and the objectives are not well defined,
5. When the research would be technically inadequate,
6. When a test does not represent reality,
7. When the information already exists, and
8. When you know what you need to know without research.

The point is that in connection with many marketing problems, research cannot make a significant contribution. A priori recognition of this fact does not diminish or tarnish the reputation of market research. It improves its reputation by minimizing after-the-fact disappointments.

Quantification

To return to our reference point, the AMA's definition of marketing research, it may be noted, includes *data* as a key word. This may be interpreted to mean that marketing research deals with information that can be organized for systematic review and statistical analysis, with information that is precise rather than ambiguous, and with information that is quantitative as opposed to qualitative.

The fact is that many studies conducted under the label of market research do not collect "data" in the usual sense of the word. Focus group interviewing is today a popular method of conducting qualitative research. This type of research is useful, on occasion. However, its use is questionable when interpreters draw conclusions well beyond their research, without appropriate caveats. This criticism aims at the use of qualitative research results and not at the methods per se.

Dissatisfaction with such methods is also rooted in the feeling that qualitative research may not readily be tested for its validity. Such research often is vague, like astrology, and subject to very personal interpretation. On the other hand, *quantification* allows for dispassionate comparison in different circumstances, leading to the ability to judge the worth of such research. Measures of purchases, or intentions, or attitudes, or whatever the research is trying to reflect, usually better allow for generalization beyond a sample.

The rejoinder of advocates of qualitative research is direct. The criterion by which to judge any research is its usefulness, especially in a business context. Does it or does it not help someone make better decisions? Its use is a personal thing, and its usefulness can be assessed qualitatively. However, most often this is more easily claimed than fulfilled.

Systematic is another key word in the aforementioned definition of marketing research. It means that there are research methods, founded on theory and principles drawn from mathematics and statistics, and psychology, and a great deal of empirical experience. This aspect of the definition should focus our attention on well thought out and carefully planned research, and away from informal, loose ill-structured attempts at fact-finding. Later we shall discuss some of these methods.

The notion that research be undertaken systematically is very important for successful applications. It is also a very challenging one. It requires careful planning through all stages of a research project, from a clear statement of the objectives to the plans for ultimate tabulations and analyses. This kind of advance thinking is always difficult, almost painful. It can rarely be done with perfection. It is more a matter of degree. But, in general, the more systematically a study is planned, the better the chances of satisfying its objectives.

Additional Issues

The AMA definition makes no explicit mention (probably in the interest of brevity) of four points worthy of some discussion:

1. the objectivity of research,
2. the quality of research,
3. the purpose of research, and
4. research methodology.

Objectivity normally is set forth as an ideal towards which research workers in all fields strive. Unbiased research is necessary. Accuracy is important. The search for truth is imperative. Green and Tull have stated:

Objectivity in research is an all-important ingredient. Marketing research has sometimes been defined as "the application of scientific method to marketing." The heart of scientific method is the objective gathering and analysis of information. Research projects that are carried out for the purpose of "proving" that a prior opinion is correct are, at best, a waste of time and resources; if research is intentionally slanted to arrive at predetermined results, a serious and inexcusable breach of ethics is involved.[6]

But, the fact is that objectivity often is an elusive notion. What is objective to one person may not be to another. Must objectivity always be a matter of subjective opinion? Much time and effort can be devoted to a discussion of the concept of objectivity without very fruitful results. Should we ignore, if not discard, the concept of objectivity in research?

Most persons would say that to abandon objectivity as a postulate of good research would do much more harm than good. Yet, an uncomfortably large proportion of what is labeled *market research* often appears to fail to be objective in either auspices, purpose, or method. How often, for example, is media research but a sales tool?

Quality of Research

Quality is another important issue in defining the limits of marketing research. There is a difficulty in raising and discussing this issue of quality. The difficulty is that the issue is well known but not often discussed. There is tremendous variation in the quality of "good" market research.

Perhaps this variation, in itself, is not bad. Quality of research, for the most part, varies directly with the quality of the researcher and the funds available for research. No one would claim that every research project can or should achieve an objective within a maximal budget. Many projects do not warrant it because their potential contribution to the decision-making process is limited.

Besides, there is a margin of uncertainty in the results of every study. Extra expenditures may reduce marginally but not eliminate that uncertainty. Thus, one can reasonably and realistically argue that good research does not always require the highest cost research.

Good market research should be viewed as that research which balances quality, risk, usefulness, and costs. The difficulty with this proposition is that precise balancing of these determinants of satisfactory research is virtually impossible. Quality, risk, and usefulness are very difficult to evaluate in any specific research application. In contrast, cost is not difficult, nor as difficult, to measure. And, hence, it often becomes the overriding consideration in re-

search. Thus, the quality of market research often is determined by default. There is a body of theory and a set of principles in research against which to assess particular practices. Some of the primary ingredients of good research are:

1. Careful planning of a study from beginning to end to coordinate the various stages of research and to minimize changes after the study has commenced;
2. Probability sampling, which means a well-structured rather than haphazard procedure for selecting a sample in a study;
3. Concerted effort in carrying out study procedures to collect the specified information from the designated sample;
4. Rigid adherence to study procedures without unnecessary improvisation on the part of personnel assigned to conduct the study; and
5. Appropriate interpretation and analysis of the results, with due regard for the margins of uncertainty in the data.

Does 2 + 2 = 4?

The last point always leads me to the question, "Does $2 + 2 = 4$ in market research?" The phrasing of this question requires some explanation.

A number of years ago, my good friend and colleague, W. Edwards Deming, and I had a conversation on the aims of education in which he expressed his opinion that students spent much of their elementary and secondary school years, and a good part of their undergraduate education, learning that 2 plus 2 equals 4. He said that the point of graduate education was to teach them that 2 plus 2 does not necessarily equal 4.

The point that Dr. Deming was making in a subtle and elegant way was that many people—far too many people—look at numbers with a naive, trusting confidence characteristic of grade school children.

Does this feeling about the question, $2 + 2 = 4$, apply in the field of marketing research? Is the accuracy of market research data of concern to people who work with such data? Is it of concern to the marketing research firms who produce such data? Or do the consumers and producers of market research explicitly or implicitly treat their data with that same naive, trusting confidence that enables the schoolboy or schoolgirl to add 2 plus 2 and always get 4?

Everyone, of course, will have to answer these questions on the basis of his own background of experience. Many researchers feel that the "2-plus-2-equals-4" phenomenon is too prevalent in the field of marketing research. A few years ago, Charles Mayer put it more directly: "The marketing research profession has been deluding its clients and itself that the work it performs is more accurate than it really is."[7]

Accuracy of Market Research

The remedy? The field could take some giant strides towards greater professionalism by working to increase levels of consciousness about the accuracy and the inaccuracies in marketing research data.

As expressed, the phenomenon implies a large measure of naivete. However, naivete or lack of sophistication is not always to blame. There are other reasons for it at times. In any case, the net effect is that the accuracy of market research data is very often ignored. To be sure, questions concerning the accuracy of data are almost always difficult to ask, and even more difficult to answer. And even when they are asked, and then answered, what is the consequence? Often, people without the proper background—or even with it— throw up their hands when confronted with information on the inaccuracies in market research data. But, dare one conclude that they are better off ignorant of such information?

Few, if any, professionals in market research would ever explicitly disagree with the desirability of knowing about the accuracy of data. Therefore, we can be hopeful that more initiative will be taken to raise consciousness levels. Marketing research as a field will ultimately profit from a greater realization that market research data are often subject to different kinds of inaccuracies, and that knowledge of such imperfections are important in deciding how much weight to give such data in decision-making activities.

Of course, as discussed earlier, in any particular circumstance, market research data may be far more accurate than is necessary, or grossly inadequate for the purpose at hand. This is a separate issue. The immediate point is that too often no one thinks about this one way or the other.

Lack of interest in accuracy seems to be the fault of both consumers and producers of data for several reasons. The blame does not fall solely with those often maligned decision-makers who use, or misuse, market research data. It even applies to many professionals in the field. Concern about accuracy does not always precede, and certainly does not always preclude, use of the most sophisticated statistical techniques on marketing data.

Other examples should occur to anyone who has the opportunity to see reports from several market research firms, including some of the most prestigious. Such reports are usually laden with many 2s and other numbers as well, providing users with many opportunities to calculate 2 plus 2. Rarely does one find adequate caveats in such reports with regard to the accuracy of the data. And, often procedures are spelled out in such little detail there is no hope for even the most astute professional to guess the level of accuracy of data.

It is, of course, insufficient to talk about sampling errors, which often are the least of the problems affecting market research data. The most troublesome studies to me are those that report standard errors as if they represented total survey error. It is certainly true, as the old saying goes, that a standard error is as bad as a nonstandard error. But, it surely doesn't represent the only kind.

Why is there so little attention paid to the accuracy of market research data? One answer may center on a lack of sophistication in our society when it comes to statistics or to numbers in general.

A second reason for inattentiveness to errors is the competitive nature of the market research industry. Do we expect a firm to expose or even to highlight the weaknesses in its product, when its competitors may be less open? How easy it is, in these circumstances, to ignore an issue that most everyone finds distasteful anyway. As anyone who has worked in marketing research knows, it is a fiercely competitive field, in which the consumers of services are extremely cost-conscious. A great deal of market research is bought by people with very limited technical backgrounds with which to assess the quality of research. And, in fairness, many admit this quite openly. As mentioned earlier, the result is, in very many cases, that cost considerations overwhelm quality considerations. This setting makes it very difficult for producers not to ignore considerations of accuracy.

There is a third reason for the lack of interest in accuracy. Perhaps little attention is paid because even when information on accuracy is available, it is not clear how such information can be directly useful. Is it really important to know something about the accuracy of market research data, and if so, why?

It is important for a user of market research data to know something about the accuracy of his data in order to conclude how much weight to give those data in making a decision and how much weight to give to judgment and to other relevant information that may be available.

What, if anything, can be done to encourage consumers and producers to consider more explicitly the accuracy of market research data?

Perhaps greater educational effort would help. Possibly more time in courses in marketing research and perhaps in marketing could be devoted to sources of error and bias in survey results. Perhaps the fundamental aim of a course in marketing research should be to bring the students to the point where they will never again look at a number with the same naive, trusting confidence that they had as grade school children.

It also seems to me a certain kind of industry effort might prove fruitful. At times, various industry groups have sought to set standards for market research. Many of these efforts are misdirected—namely, those that attempt to set performance standards. Virtually all of the performance standards I have ever seen are, to be blunt, silly. For example: "Keypunching should always be subject to 100% verification." Or: "A questionnaire should be long enough to provide the required information, but short enough to avoid respondent fatigue." I don't believe appropriate performance standards can ever be set in the field.

What would be very helpful, however, is an industry code for disclosure. Let a firm do market research any way it wishes, so long as a full report on what it does is made available to users. The objectives I would set for such a code would be directed to answer two questions:

1. What information regarding the research methodology underlying the reported data should be disclosed?
2. In what form should such information be reported and how should it be organized?

Another objective of such an effort might be to standardize terminology, in order to avoid enormous confusion. Some people use terms such as *reliability* and *accuracy* interchangeably, whereas careful practice suggests distinguishing between them. Terms like *response error* and *interviewer bias* are often used loosely, without reference to a standard against which such errors or procedural biases must be measured. The notion of true values, which is meaningless, prevails. It would be useful, I feel, to try to conform usage and at least to eliminate confusion on accuracy of data that arises from loose talk and semantic differences.

The scope of disclosure for marketing research ideally would be wide, covering four main areas: (1) the nature of the data being reported; (2) the statistical population and sample selection; (3) survey methods, operations and procedures; and (4) accuracy and reliability of survey results.

The latter in particular, would be helpful in forcing a user of market research to focus on the accuracy of his data. Actually, information on all of these subjects would contribute to a better appreciation of the limits of market research, and hopefully to greater recognition that such limits exist that will, in the long run, benefit the profession.

THE PURPOSE OF RESEARCH

One concept, obscured by the definition of marketing research adopted as a focal point for our discussion, is particularly important and relevant. The definition fails explicitly to relate research to its ultimate use. Every book written these days in marketing research addresses this omission.

One leading marketing research textbook by Boyd and Westfall states, "The purpose of any marketing research is to provide information which will enable the identification and solution of a marketing problem."[8]

Historically, research was thought of as a search for knowledge or "studious inquiry," as one of the dictionaries referenced earlier still calls it. This point of view focuses on obtaining facts from figures, on deriving conclusions from research effort, and on increasing knowledge. Research in this view is a learning experience. And so it still is. But in recent years a school of thought has emerged that relates research and research methods to ultimate uses of the research.

This "new" pragmatic philosophy might be briefly stated as follows: The purpose of research is not merely to learn something; the purpose is to provide a guide to action in one or more specific problem situations. It is learning for a purpose.

This philosophy of research as a guide to action is, of course, not a truth. It is merely a point of view. Most market researchers would, I think, agree that it is a good point of view or philosophy under which to operate. This means paying more than lip service to the philosophy. It is, however, not always easy to do so. Let's consider some reasons why research is not always explicitly action oriented.

Fundamental Versus Applied Research

Two categories of market research, fundamental research and applied research, should be separated. Fundamental or basic or pure research aims to extend the boundaries of knowledge in an area, with no immediate applications to existing problems. Much of it is methodological, that is, research on methods that are or can be used in market research. So there is an ultimate use, but not necessarily an immediate business decision that will be affected by the research.

Virtually everyone agrees that there is a great need in marketing for more fundamental research. This is especially true in the area of consumer behavior. Without greater knowledge of how and why consumers of goods and services behave as they do, how can there be intelligent marketing decisions? Yet we know so little about consumer behavior, at least judging by our ability to predict that behavior. Much, much more fundamental research is needed. But consumer behavior is not always a fruitful area in which to do research. There is at least some measure of truth to Hartley's statement:

The consumer, whether householder or industrial purchaser, should be the focus of marketing efforts. . . . In an effort to understand consumers better and influence them favorably, marketers are conducting a huge amount of research into customer decision making. However, so far the study of consumer behavior has shown primarily how really complex this subset of human behavior is.[9]

The concept of research as a guide to action might be thought more appropriate to applied rather than to fundamental research. Not so, some argue. Thinking through the ultimate uses of any piece of research should influence the design of that research and, hopefully, make it more useful. Merely thinking of research as "adding to knowledge" results in much that is interesting, but not necessarily useful.

Applied marketing research is an attempt to acquire knowledge to help reach a decision for an immediate problem or set of problems. The use of research as a guide to action seems like a very natural philosophy under which to conduct applied marketing research. It almost seems unnatural for research to be conducted in a business organization for any other reason.

However, the way in which marketing research contributes to marketing decisions is often very indirect—and often obscure. We don't fully understand the process under which a marketing decision-maker adds research to his prior intuition, judgment, and experience, and then synthesizes this conglomerate of facts and feeling into a decision.

The best, most carefully thought-out applied marketing research study proceeds somewhat along the following lines. A product manager faces a problem such as whether to introduce a new consumer product. He asks himself what he would like to know. A partial enumeration includes such things as the number of consumers that comprise the potential market, some demographic characteristics of those consumers and their location, buying habits of such consumers, current competition for the product, longer-term as well as short-term prospects for the product, and so on and so forth. A consumer research study is drafted, hopefully in consultation with someone from the marketing research department. The study is conducted and the results processed, tabulated, and summarized. The product manager then reviews the results, digests some, throws others away, and reaches a conclusion on what actions to take. Did the research contribute to the decision? Possibly. How was it used? This is the mysterious process we know relatively little about in marketing. Marketing decision processes are mostly informal, intuitive, subjective, instinctive and judgmental—whether research is involved or not.

Again, we should stress that this certainly does not mean that most marketing decisions are poor, nor does it necessarily mean that many marketing decisions could be improved by more formal decision procedures. Notice that the question we have raised is, "How was the research used?" The even deeper question is, "How should it be used?"

This line of questioning is raised for only one reason: to stress that the real potential of research is difficult to realize when decision-making is informal. The more precise the decision process, the more precise the research contribution can be.

My model situation, if anything, probably overstates the precision with which most marketing managers think through their research needs. In most companies, the market research director's lament begins with the query: "What do you want to know?" And, as the joke goes, "Why do you need it yesterday?"

How much responsibility should the market researcher take in defining the information needs of a marketing problem? An even broader issue is how much responsibility the market researcher should assume in the full decision-making process. There can be no absolute rules in this area. So much depends on the people involved, their abilities, their backgrounds, their attitudes, and how they interact.

Despite the difficulty of generalization, my judgment is that normally the more involved a market researcher is in a decision problem, the more successful his research is likely to be. If the researcher assumes only a passive role in the process of using research, the chances for successful application are more limited.

Small and Rosenberg have made an interesting study as to how the marketing researcher perceives himself as a decision-maker and how he is perceived by marketing managers. They point out, first, that popular images are:

Researchers are typically satisfied with a nominal role in management decision making; moreover, they typically avoid decision responsibilities.

Researchers typically perceive participation in decision activity as increasing interpersonal conflicts with marketing managers.

Marketing managers at the middle management level (e.g., product managers) are typically dissatisfied with the performance of researchers who expand their decision-making role.[10]

However, on the basis of their study, Small and Rosenberg feel there is at least some evidence that challenges these beliefs. They tentatively conclude that "most researchers accept some decision responsibility" and "the majority of researchers who accept some decision responsibility experience higher job performance evaluations, more job satisfaction, and less role conflict with marketing managers than those researchers who avoid decision making."

Focusing solely on the market researcher and his role in the decision-making process is, of course, insufficient. The role of the marketing manager in formulating research is equally as important for successful uses of research. This means more than having the marketing manager involved in deciding on the informational needs of his problem. His involvement should extend to understanding the research methodology to be employed, its limitations, and the kinds of uncertainties surrounding the data it will generate. A long-run aim in the field of marketing education should be to turn out marketing managers with ever better research backgrounds.

This discussion of the use of research for marketing decisions naturally leads to consideration of marketing decision-making in general, wholly apart from the question of how research is used in that process. There would be many benefits from better understanding of marketing decision processes, leading to greater formalization of such processes. Just from a research point of view, there would be tremendous advantages in enabling the design of sharper, more relevant, and more useful research.

This is perhaps futuristic. It certainly is not in the present. Marketing research is used mostly in an informal way to contribute to strategy decisions in marketing. It contributes to knowledge and in this sense it is blended, albeit in ways unknown, with judgment, experience, and intuition—hopefully with the result of somewhat better decisions. This is not the ideal setting in which to practice research, but that is the way it is, at least for now.

RESEARCH METHODOLOGY

We once again return to the question, "What is market research?" for discussion of one last dimension: research methodology. This is an important dimension. As Boyd and Westfall state: "A definition of marketing research must also stress *how* the data are obtained and evaluated."[11] This requires special techniques or methods. The study of methods is a significant part of any course in marketing research, whether measured in terms of time spent, degree of difficulty, or importance.

There is a variety of methods used in market research. One ends up with somewhat different lists depending on how he wishes to define and classify various methods. A mutually exclusive and collectively exhaustive list of methods will not be attempted here because it would serve little purpose. Rather we shall review a few miscellaneous, yet significant issues, connected with certain market research methods:

1. The market survey,
2. Marketing experiments, and
3. Multivariate methods.

The Market Survey

The most widely used technique in applied market research is the survey. Surveys can and often are directed at business units, particularly in industrial marketing where those units are the ultimate consumers. But most survey work is consumer research directed at households or individual persons residing in households. While such consumer surveys may involve only direct or indirect observation (e.g., via a television metering device or a pantry check), most of them involve asking people questions. In fact the term *survey* usually connotes only that kind of study: going out and asking people questions.

For better or for worse the survey has become an American institution. Virtually every day of the year (except perhaps for Christmas and Mother's Day) the survey research process goes forward. Squads of personal interviewers are regularly dispatched to apartments, homes, or shopping centers. Telephone interviewers sit at phones at home or in central locations and dial designated numbers. Clerks stuff questionnaires, with or without incentives, to be dispatched via the mails throughout the country. In short, the survey, a method developed over the past forty years, is being used by managers and planners throughout the United States and gives every appearance of being here to stay.

Not all survey work is marketing research. Public opinion polls and other kinds of social surveys add to the total. No precise data are available, but it is likely that marketing or marketing-related problems account for a very large proportion of surveys conducted in this country. I say this with the private sector of the economy primarily in mind, but it is also true to a large extent for survey research conducted by the public sector.

Why the continuing growth in survey research? What is its appeal? The natural answer is given eloquently by Warwick and Lininger:

> The growth of surveys and other types of social research in the twentieth century is closely tied to a heightened emphasis upon the values of knowledge and rationality. The experimental and problem-solving attitude that undergirds scientific and technological progress has carried over to the social sphere as well. Modern man wishes to deal with situations in which he is an actor by developing plans based upon *solid information.* Although this ideal is often unrealized, the value placed on "getting the facts" is very much a part of contemporary culture. The survey is increasingly seen as a helpful method of collecting information on socially relevant topics.[12][emphasis added]

It is easy to say many good things about the survey from the point of view of the research person. The theory of probability sampling has been highly developed and widely applied. It serves as a very powerful tool in the design of surveys. Also a good deal is known, from a great deal of experience, about questionnaire design and appropriate ways of doing field work.

One should not imply that all the technical problems associated with surveys are easily overcome. And one should certainly not imply that most surveys are done well. Much survey work leaves a lot to be desired. The point is, however, that the market survey is one area of marketing where there is good theory and sound principles on how to do the job well. All it takes is time, money, effort, and competence.

The survey, properly done, normally provides the two ingredients of objective research: (1) quantitative measurements that allow for dispassionate comparisons, unrelated to the comparer; and (2) the ability to replicate that allows us to have confidence that research results are not statistical aberrations, peculiar to the person who conducted the research at the particular time it was conducted. In brief, survey information can be solid. The technology is there.

To claim this as an advantage assumes, of course, that survey research does, in fact, provide solid information for the decision-maker, or the actor as Warwick and Lininger call him. This assumption is to be questioned in at least some cases. And, in other cases, the relevance and usefulness of survey results, even if they are "solid," are in doubt. Some writers attribute negative value to surveys or "popularity polls," as they are often disparagingly called in these circumstances. Television ratings, one of the best known forms of market research, are an example of occasional tirades in this direction.

At this point, I would like to interject a proposition. The survey cannot be viewed merely as a tool with which the market researcher can find interesting and enlightening facts about his product or service. The survey must contribute to society, and the market research profession will have to do a better job about documenting such contributions in the future. Surveys often are the subject of citizen complaints that they represent a public nuisance. Society's growing concern about invasion of privacy is moving ever closer to the survey profession[13]. We hear now the charge that certain favorite marketing questions invade privacy. We may well ultimately hear the charge that the act of survey solicitation itself is such an invasion. This is sure to happen if and when society recognizes that a very large percentage of marketing research deals much more with advertising strategy than with other product questions. And, in any case, recent years have seen some erosion in the public's willingness to participate, particularly in surveys conducted by personal interview.

A wide variety of different kinds of information are collected by marketing research surveys. Much survey work is relatively straightforward in attempting to collect data on past or current consumer behavior. Such questions may include the following: Which brand of a product was purchased last time? Who in the household was primarily responsible for the decision to buy? Who in the household will use the product? At which outlet was the product purchased? How did the purchaser become interested or familiar with the product, and so forth?

Design of a survey to collect behavioral information is easily relative to other problems in market research. Difficulties occur in two areas: (1) deciding exactly what kind of information to collect; and (2) technical problems (e.g., sampling and questionnaire design) in actually collecting it. But when the results are in, one more or less knows, conceptually, what he has.

This is not often the case in studies that deal with other than behavioral information—with intentions or attitudes or opinions. Information on intentions, for example, is intuitively appealing to most market researchers and marketing managers as well. The essence of this type of inquiry is (1) what do you plan to do? or (2) what will you do *if?* or (3) what would you do *if?* Different levels of sophistication can be heaped on this line of questioning, for example, by making the inquiry in terms of "how likely" a certain action or decision is. Intentions data are often collected in consumer research and are often disappointing in their predictive ability. It is hard to give up on this one, but the burden is on the market researcher, in any given application, to answer two tough issues: Can consumers predict their own behavior? Can they answer hypothetical questions?

Attitudinal and opinion data present even a tougher set of issues. The logic underlying their extensive use in market research is that attitudes affect consumer decisions and it is, therefore, important that the marketing man know what those attitudes are, how they change, and how they are influenced. As a general proposition this seems reasonable. But, do attitudes influence market behavior in a given marketing problem? What attitudes are relevant? Can they be measured? Attitudinal data are the most difficult types of marketing information to obtain, but this is overshadowed by the difficulty of interpreting and acting upon them.

Test Marketing

What is an alternative to the survey process? One covered extensively in marketing research books is the field experiment—test marketing. This has been characterized as the "wave of the future" in research, but unfortunately it has held that label for years. The concept of experimentation is an appealing one: Don't ask. Don't infer. Actually see how the consumer, or whoever, reacts in a situation which simulates or even mirrors reality.

Of course, as many people have discovered, it is not quite that easy for several reasons:

1. It is often difficult to simulate reality in terms of market areas, seasons, products, and so forth—all of which make generalizations tenuous, if not difficult.
2. There normally are large amounts of apparently uncontrollable variations in marketing problems, which necessitate fairly large-scale experiments to measure effects with precision.
3. Experiments usually are quite expensive in two dimensions: (a) the real cost in terms of conducting the study; and (b) perceived opportunity loss from experimenting in a market rather than continuing present marketing strategy.

These barriers are admittedly difficult ones to overcome in specific problem situations. However, bona fide experimentation provides the most sound basis for marketing decisions and the development of marketing theory. So it is to be hoped that this area of applied market research will grow.

Multivariate Methods

Any discussion of methods in marketing research, however brief, would be woefully incomplete without some reference to multivariate methods and their use. These methods include regression analysis, discriminant analysis, factor analysis, multidimensional scaling, cluster analysis, and canonical analysis. They all have a noble and worthwhile aim: to help the researcher boil down the masses of data he is faced with. Data reduction is a formidable job. Multivariate methods provide the computer with procedures for doing this boil-down in logical and meaningful ways.

It seems that the marketing jury is still out on multivariate methods. There are many advocates, some of whom can trot out a number of interesting, perhaps even useful, applications. But there are also many technically competent researchers who are less enthusiastic. Criticisms are of many kinds and are leveled at multivariate applications and certainly not at the methods themselves. Critics often derisively will use the phrase *a technique in search of a problem* to stress the fact that such techniques do not find natural application in marketing. Often the interpretation of the results of a multivariate analysis is highly subjective, and extends far beyond the research itself. In fact, one may occasionally wonder what, if any, contribution the research made at all. Are these applications objective? Are they subject to replication? And, if not, are they to be evaluated on some criterion?

Conclusion

For the last time, I return to the question, "What is market research?" The question is not precisely answerable, and never will be, because it leads to so many other difficult questions and issues. But nonetheless, the foregoing analysis includes one point: The question, "What is market research?" is worth asking again, and again, and again.

NOTES

1. Robert J. Small and Larry J. Rosenberg, "The Marketing Researcher As a Decision Maker: Myth or Reality?" *Journal of Marketing* (January 1975): pp. 2-7. Based on Dik W. Twedt, *A Survey of Marketing Research* (Chicago: American Marketing Association, 1974).

2. *Report of the Definitions Committee of the American Marketing Association* (Chicago: American Marketing Association, 1961).

3. Harper W. Boyd, Jr. and Ralph Westfall, *Marketing Research*, Third Edition (Homewood: R. D. Irwin, 1972), p. 6.

4. Henry Assael and A. Marvin Roscoe, Jr., "Approaches to Market Segmentation Analysis," *Journal of Marketing* (October 1976): p. 67.

5. Lee Adler, "A 'Dissident' View on Market Research," *CMC Monograph Series*, (Princeton: Center for Marketing Communications, 1975).

6. Paul Green and Donald S. Tull, *Research for Marketing Decisions*, Third Edition, (Englewood Cliffs: Prentice-Hall, 1975), p. 5.

7. Charles Mayer, "Assessing the Accuracy of Marketing Research," *Journal of Marketing Research* (August 1970): p. 285.

8. Boyd and Westfall, *Marketing Research*, p. 4. See also Green and Tull, *Marketing Decisions*, p. 4, and Donald S. Tull and Del I. Hawkins, *Marketing Research* (New York: Macmillan, 1976), p. 3.

9. Robert F. Hartley, *Marketing Fundamentals for Responsive Management* (New York: Dun-Donnelly, 1976), p. 121.

10. Small and Rosenberg, "Marketing Researcher," pp. 2, 6, 7.

11. Boyd and Westfall, *Marketing Research*, p. 4.

12. Donald P. Warwick and Charles A. Lininger, *The Sample Survey: Theory and Practice* (New York: McGraw-Hill, 1975).

13. Alice M. Tybout and Gerald Zaltman, "Ethics in Marketing Research: Their Practical Relevance," *Journal of Marketing Research* (November 1974): pp. 357-68 and "Confidentiality of Statistical and Research Data," *Statistical Reporter* (January 1977): pp. 115-36.

SIX

Developing Marketing Strategies

in Financial Institutions

Thomas R. Wilcox

Chairman and Chief Executive Officer
Crocker National Bank

It would please the professors I had at New York University in the early 1930s to know that during the course of a forty-two-year career in banking there have been many, many occasions when I have called upon a banking principle or fact gleaned when I was a student at NYU.

In the light of recent economic history some turn out to be quite prophetic. For example:

1. That a commercial bank is a merchant of debt, and, therefore, most vulnerable and responsive to business cycles.
2. That the commercial bank function is essentially passive in the sense that it cannot "sell a loan"; it can only respond to a customer's need and initiative. I should add, however, that a bank marketing executive can profit by investigating what it is that makes a customer "buy" a loan, when, and from whom.
3. That the balance sheets of both the borrower and the banker are the essential cornerstones of an effective financial relationship.

These three fundamentals seem to me as valid today as they were forty years ago and will be equally as valid forty years from now.

Parenthethically, I recall some other "fundamentals" I was taught there that have not turned out to be quite as valid or permanent. For example:

1. That with respect to government bonds the price would never fall below par because the integrity of government would never permit it. I recall that among the first and most classic falls of government bonds below par was the break in 1951 of the 2 1/2s of 67/72. They fell, as I recall, into the low 80s.
2. That with respect to railroads, their perpetual survival is insured by the simple fact that their rights of way are not duplicable and that they are natural monopolies.

MARKETING STRATEGY DEFINED

My experience suggests that marketing strategy may be defined as a continuously changing plan to satisfy requirements for goods or services within the market selected, that the market dimension be optimally defined, that the delivery of the product or service produce relatively equal short- and long-term benefits to the supplier and to the buyer, and that the plan be designed to survive violent and unexpected change in the economic environment.

Marketing strategy, therefore, is nothing other than the combined answers to the questions concerning what markets we are to serve, with what product or service, at what price, with what investment in advertising and promotion, to what level of sales, and with what profit consequences.

I should also define exactly what kind of financial institutions we will be talking about. Financial institutions range from large life insurance companies to the smudgy check-cashing windows of Chicago's money shops. For our purposes, I am talking about financial intermediaries: those institutions engaged in the business of gathering or creating funds in large and small amounts, pooling them, and lending them to, or bringing them to, the point of purchase for creditworthy borrowers.

Commercial banks do all that the specialized institutions like savings banks do, and more. Consequently, development of marketing strategy for commercial banks is more complex than for those institutions which specialize. For that reason, plus the fact that almost my entire business career has been in commercial banking, my discussion here will focus on the complexities of market strategy development in commercial banking. Much of it might apply, however, to other kinds of financial institutions.

My thesis here is that, though the market planning process in a financial institution may be the same as in any other, the actual strategy developed is profoundly influenced by the fact that banks are instrumentalities of the monetary system and important conduits of economic policy. They are repositories of other people's funds charged with responsibility for keeping the wheels of commerce turning. These basic facts of banking life call for a high degree of adaptability to economic conditions as well as obedience to government regulation.

Evolution of Banking

The history of banking over the last forty years is but a history of adaptation to changing markets and a changing business environment. Let me sketch it for you.

The establishment of the Federal Reserve System in 1913 brought the banking industry under the general control of a central bank. But the nature and application of central banking practices in the early years of the Fed were viewed as inadequate in light of the great depression of the 1930s.

The monetary and economic turmoil of the 1930s resulted in reform legislation aimed at overhauling the nation's financial system. The legislative names are familiar: including the Glass-Steagall Act of 1933, the Securities Act of 1933, the Securities and Exchange Act of 1934, and the Banking Act of 1935. To a large extent, the legal and regulatory environment within which the banking system operates today is based upon the "reforms" of forty years ago.

The reforms of the 1930s were primarily aimed at improving and preserving the integrity of the banking system and protecting the public. The stability of the system since then indicates that the changes were, in this sense, well founded. Unfortunately, this banking structure did not always provide the framework for aggressive growth appropriate to the economic expansion of the postwar period. Consequently, banks have responded with new services and new structures which have tended to shape at least some modification in the regulations.

During the 1940s the banks in this country mounted a massive effort to accommodate the financial requirements of industry and government. Then, beginning in 1945 banks were required to adjust to a long period of excessive liquidity created by wartime government financing and the financing of industrial and consumer demand built up during the war.

Bank's Marketing Strategy

If there was a marketing strategy in the immediate postwar years it was a simple strategy calling for getting money employed. Banks were excessively liquid, deposits were plentiful, and loan demand was strong. In 1946, the commercial paper rate was 5/8%, the prime 1 1/2%. Where I worked, we made several term loans at 1.85% for eight years to prime credits.

Beginning in the mid-1950s and on through the decade of the 1960s most banks did, in fact, begin to develop what may be regarded as long-term and more meaningful marketing strategies. In that period, banks required a continuous supply of low-cost funds to accommodate credit demanded by both business and individual borrowers, although bank and industrial liquidity was declining.

Branch expansion became a major part of that effort. In 1950 U.S. commercial banks had some 5,000 branch locations, and during that decade the number doubled to approximately 10,000. By 1965 there were 16,000 branches. Their primary function was to accumulate deposits from both individual consumers as well as businesses while lending officers ranged ever farther to satisfy the credit requirements of a burgeoning business community and a steadily increasing population.

Also gaining momentum was the advent of the holding company intended by its practitioners to find other nonbank sources of funds and outlets for new forms of credit extension. Transamerica's acquisition of Occidental Life, and a large string of banks was the archtype of an emerging marketing strategy which, as you recall, was curbed but not aborted by the Holding Company Act of 1956. I submit that the concepts and activities of those early holding companies were in the best tradition of banks as financial intermediaries.

During the decade of the 1960s, while the demand for loans was doubling in a ten-year period, traditional sources of low-cost funds continued to fail to keep pace. The relatively low-cost corporate demand deposit segment grew only moderately while the more expensive time deposit segment grew more rapidly. In that period we saw demand for loans growing at a compounded rate of approximately 10% a year while the compounded growth of demand deposits was less than 4%, and time and savings deposits grew from about a 4% annual rate to more than 10% by 1970.

This change in deposit mix and in loan demand was characterized by a substantial swing from corporate to individual deposits, another reason for building branch systems. For example, in the five-year period 1968-73 for the entire commercial banking system, individuals supplied $164 billion in deposits while corporations supplied only $22 billion. At the same time individuals drew only $67 billion in loans and business customers drew $110 billion. Stated differently, individuals were net providers of $97 billion of funds while businesses were net users of $88 billion of funds. Clearly the individual depositor became and still is today the major source of core deposits for the banking system. And this state of affairs will continue while Regulation Q is in force.

By the end of the decade of the 1960s bankers were facing the fact that more costly interest-bearing funds were rapidly replacing demand deposits as the prime funds source, and a burgeoning savings banking industry was attacking the conventional time deposit voraciously. To attract funds, banks turned first to their branch systems through which they tapped individual deposits. Then they invented negotiable certificates of deposit in denominations of $100,000 and over to extract what could still be available from corporations within the restrictions of Regulation Q, and finally turned to Euro-dollars as sources of funds.

Then the pendulum began to swing back the other way. Having learned how to attract—indeed, buy—all the funds they needed, bank marketing strategy focused on where to lend the funds. Banks had traditionally financed foreign trade, but now they turned to actually lending money abroad to foreign corporate customers, to foreign banks, and to foreign governments—a whole new market strategy.

Recent years have seen other significant changes in the banking environment that should be mentioned to give you a proper historic perspective.

The "Business" of Banking

The first is that beginning in the mid-1960s—some may fix the date earlier—major banks began to view themselves as being in the "business" of banking. The rationale was, and I accept it, that to keep pace with a growing economy and with expanded requirements for banking services and bank loans, banks needed to act more like businesses; viz., they needed to have rather continuous access to the capital markets because their collective rates of growth were larger than their own internal capital generation would support. Indeed, bankers felt compelled to commit themselves publicly, as business does, to annual growth and earnings rates of 13 to 15%. And, remarkably, banks are achieving them. Another principal ingredient of a business is a requirement for large numbers of bright, new, and talented people. To attract them, banks had to promise growth, opportunity, and compensation schemes at least as rewarding as those offered by industry. So, emphasis in the banking business and market planning turned to profit.

I don't see anything wrong in this. Indeed, the federal examiners of banks today look at four significant measures of bank performance in this order: (1) management competence, (2) profitability, (3) liquidity, and (4) capital adequacy. Twenty-five years ago, the quality of management was taken for granted and bank examiners looked at the other three measures in reverse order: capital first, liquidity second, and profitability last.

Since growth and diversification are thought to be routes to more profitable ends many banks adopted, as a matter of marketing strategy, a one bank holding company mode which, until 1970, was free of regulation. The 1970 amendments to the Holding Company Act brought all bank holding companies under Federal regulation and since that date the pace of holding company formation has slowed.

Finally, of course, the malaise that has beset all business and individuals, namely inflation, has also beset financial institutions. Inflation has eroded the real value of our assets and ballooned all items of noninterest expense from salaries and occupancy to travel and advertising.

As we look at the banking environment today, the need to reassess and adapt marketing strategies to environmental realities continues. Nor can such adaptation be limited to a single area of banking activity. It must uniformly be applied to all markets one chooses to serve. Our recent experience at Crocker can well serve as an illustration. We have attempted to adapt marketing strategies to opportunities as we have encountered them in various markets, including retail, corporate, and international. Always, however, the strategies have had to be developed within the limitations of the resources, human and economic, with which we had to work at the time.

For example, a couple of years ago, we saw an opportunity to capture a larger share of the California retail market and established a strategy to change essentially the public's perception of Crocker from that of an inward-looking conservative organization to one that recognized that disgruntled customers were sometimes correct in assuming that large banks were frequently too big and too busy to care about them. Our strategy was to initiate activities that would result in the public's recogniton of us as a forward-looking institution with the needs of its customers always in the forefront. We implemented this strategy through a number of highly visible actions, beginning with the extension of our branch daily working hours from the old schedule of 10-3, to a new one of 8:30 to 4:30. These longer hours—which added only a little to our operating costs—did attract new customers and began to change public attitudes towards us as a retail institution.

At the same time, we began the process of restructuring some of our retail services to meet better the needs of specific customer groups such as senior citizens, for whom we eliminated all checking account service charges, while also creating new convenient service packages for younger groups such as college students.

We also raised our passbook savings rates to the maximum legal rate of 5% instead of the 4 1/2% which all but one major bank had been offering in California. We had no expectation that this move would attract deposits, for as anticipated, all California banks followed suit immediately. We raised the rate because to pay less than the legal maximum was not, in our view, consistent with our marketing strategy, calling for giving the best possible service to our retail customers. Not to pay the best rate would, we believe, have destroyed our credibility in the marketplace.

Since then we have pursued our strategy by announcing various services, all responsive to recognized public needs, many designed to offer competitive advantage.

At the same time that we employed a new strategy in the retail market, we also reevaluated our position in the corporate market and formulated a new strategy there. Briefly, it called for combining traditional commercial banking functions with some services typically offered by investment bankers. A commercial bank can engage in many investment banking functions which are legal under federal law. Yet, banks have largely abrogated them to the investment bankers. While we have no intention to underwrite or sell corporate equity issues, we can materially contribute to the health and prosperity of our corporate clients by having capabilities to arrange mergers, divestitures, acquisitions, private placements, or capital restructuring.

To us it seems entirely logical that this kind of service be available to a corporate customer from a commercial bank. It is the commercial banker who lives with the corporation year in and year out, understanding the customer's needs and being held accountable by the customer for the results of recommendations that are implemented. The investment banker, on the other hand, has a much more transient relationship with the customer, becoming involved only when special problems or special needs arise. To provide these services to our corporate customers we established a corporate finance department in our Corporate Banking Division staffed by individuals drawn from Wall Street investment banking houses. Some of these persons were so investment banking oriented that we provided special training for them to orient them to commercial banking functions.

Moreover, to serve the corporate market in a contemporary manner we have sought also to achieve close cooperation between our Corporate and International banking divisions. In many situations they serve the same customer who views himself as a customer of Crocker, not as a customer of a division.

To accomplish this, it was necessary also to reevaluate the marketing strategy of our International Division. We have chosen to achieve our goals abroad by acting more as an architect of financial services, geared to the overseas needs of our corporate clientele, rather than attempting to outcompete bigger banks purely on distribution strength. Accordingly, unlike some of our major competitors, we have chosen not to make massive investments in overseas facilities and personnel, but rather to provide our services to overseas corporate clients by taking better advantage of solid, long-standing relationships with foreign correspondent banks. We believe that we cannot, and should not, try to displace the in-country expertise of local banks overseas, but rather that we should meet the total needs of our customers by blending our capabilities with the strengths of our correspondents.

We do maintain overseas branches in key foreign markets like London and Tokyo, and we have representative offices in other strategic overseas locations. We manage our overseas business through relatively few area specialists located in our U.S. headquarters. Consequently, managers of our international activity can work closely with their counterparts in the Corporate Division. Through this blending we can help our clients better here, as well as overseas, without fragmenting the relationship. To date, this strategy seems successful, for we are able to increase our international business and compete effectively on the basis of service without a major overseas branch network or the problems associated with a widely dispersed management group.

And for any of us in commercial banking, the need for such adaptations continues to be undiminished.

For example, the electronic transfer of funds is already technically accomplished. It requires only the right kind of market planning to bring it into the common usage. Adapting to it will provoke a variety of changes in the way banks do business and in the cost and price of our services.

A second development on the horizon today is that the specialized financial institutions like mutual savings banks, savings and loans, and credit unions which have long functioned alongside commercial banks as specialists are now becoming generalists and more directly competitive. They are no longer exclusively thrift institutions. They are bidding to become full service banking institutions.

If you are planning bank marketing strategy in today's competitive environment, it is important to understand that there are now two distinct kinds of players on the field each playing under different rules. One group is the private financial institution, the other is the mutual. The rules by which each plays make a major competitive difference.

For example, a mutual institution is not required to keep reserves with the Federal Reserve. It is not required to file 10Ks or any other kind of report with the SEC. It usually has a self-perpetuating board. In Illinois, commercial banks are not allowed to have more than one office and even off-premises automated terminals are prohibited to commercial banks, but branches of savings and loans are abundant.

In this kind of market environment, commercial banks will no longer be able to thrive by following a marketing strategy that calls only for response to economic and business trends. Marketing strategy now and in the future will demand more initiative and better means of meeting head-to-head competition.

It is likely, too, that we may soon have a basic change in the bank regulatory structure, the first since the 1930s.

Finally, as the time span between important changes in the economic, regulatory, and competitive environments of banking institutions gets shorter and shorter, the lead time required to "redirect the bank" gets longer and longer.

FACTORS IN MARKET PLANNING

Anticipating change and adapting to it becomes an increasingly important part of the banker's task. Market planning is more essential than ever to success in the banking business. But market planning in any economic environment and against any anticipated developments must always observe four basic fundamentals that are unique to banking. If they are not observed and accommodated, the plan will be worthless and the institution possibly imperiled.

The first and most important principle is that a banker is a fiduciary. By that I mean that a banker's inventory belongs to his depositors. The most important element in the banking loop are the depositors. It is their money and they have a right to it at any time.

Banks are licensed by law to serve as repositories of citizens' funds and to use those funds for constructive purposes. No sound bank marketing strategy can ignore or escape that requirement.

Second, and this of course follows from the first, a banker is expected to minimize risk before maximizing return. That is just a fancy way of saying that a banker is expected to get back the money he or she lends. Fundamental, yes, but often overlooked in the decade of the sixties when traditional good credit judgment was often submerged in a tide of opinion that nothing could fail, that all new ventures were good ventures, and that cash flow mattered more than balance sheet analyses.

This is where I return to one of the fundamentals I learned at New York University forty years ago. A banker is a merchant of debt. The banker's assets are his customer's liabilities. Consequently, the integrity of the balance sheet of both the borrower and the banker must be preserved if the financial relationship between the two is to be rewarding. Bankers have sometimes forgotten this principle and in doing so have fostered economic tragedies.

I believe the failure of the Penn Central and the W. T. Grant organizations may be cases in point. Had the bankers been as concerned about the integrity of those balance sheets and their supporting schedules as they should have been, those tragedies might have been avoided.

The banker must always ask, "Am I doing good with the money I lend? Is the loan I am making likely to improve the economic health of the borrower, or is it likely to encourage the borrower to dissipation? Is our new emphasis on profits undermining our analysis of the real risk?"

Since bankers are merchants of debt, bank market planning must take cognizance of the fact that the purchase of debt or—if you prefer—the lending of money, must always be made in response to an expressed need of the customer. You cannot, in my opinion, successfully employ a marketing strategy that attempts to create a market for debt where one does not legitimately exist.

Many of us in banking have personal knowledge of situations where our lack of discipline and our failure to be fiduciaries have contributed to the delinquency and resulting failure of borrowers. Real Estate Investment Trusts are excellent cases in point.

Finally, banks must stand ready to serve their markets in bad times as well as good. Loans must be made whether interest rates are low or high, whether the spread is narrow or wide. Foreign trade must be financed; interest must be paid to depositors; municipal bonds must be underwritten. In short, the wheels of commerce must be kept turning. A bank has a franchise to serve the public. An industrial marketing executive can cut his losses and take a product off the market if it is unprofitable. Bankers cannot decide to stop accepting deposits or making loans, though they can and must control the pace of both.

Bankers' marketing strategy must accommodate continuance in the market of the full spectrum of the essential services a bank provides under all business conditions.

CONSTRAINTS OF GOVERNMENT REGULATION

All bank market planning must, of course, accommodate itself to the constraints of government regulation.

There are three good reasons why banks are properly subject to government regulation.

First, these institutions have a franchise or responsibility to serve commerce and industry in a variety of ways without which our economy would become inert.

Second, financial institutions deal with and serve almost every individual in this country. There is very little money left in mattresses anymore.

Finally, the commercial banking system is especially cloaked with the public interest because it has the power to create money, and does so when it makes loans and buys government securities. Indeed, it is worth noting that it is the commercial banks that have been buying, and monetizing, a large portion of the growing government debt.

Therefore, market planning in a financial institution, perforce, continually bumps against regulatory boundaries. Interest rate ceilings affect pricing strategy. Restrictions on branching affect distribution strategy. Reserve requirements affect lending strategy. Nevertheless, this is all in the public interest and while often inappropriately executed, government regulation is entirely appropriate in principle.

The problem, therefore, is not the fact of government regulation; it is the character and the quality of it. The deficiency of both is traceable, I believe, to a couple of causes I would like to describe briefly.

The first cause is the rampant proliferation of agencies claiming regulatory privilege. We are faced with a bureaucracy of overlapping and competing jurisdictions at city, state, and federal levels that is oppressive and expensive to us and to the public at large.

General Motors may not be a typical case, but they have made an estimate of the cost to them to comply with government regulations last year: it totaled $1.3 billion. This is more than it cost to operate the entire federal government during the first seventy-five years of this country's existence. More to the point, it is more than twice what GM spent for plant and equipment in 1974. And only twice in the last ten years have dividend payments on GM common stock exceeded that amount.

Many companies, of which we at Crocker are one, are beginning to reckon the total cost of compliance with proliferating rules. Senator Percy is compiling data, and I suspect his findings will be astounding.

Banks are answerable to the traditional bank regulatory authorities: the Comptroller of the Currency, the Federal Reserve Board, the Federal Deposit Insurance Corporation, and State Banking Commissioners. But we are also answerable to the Securities and Exchange Commission, to the Treasury Department, to the Labor Department, to the Internal Revenue Service, to the Department of Justice, and recently the Federal Trade Commission has asserted authority. Couple those with city, state, and sometimes county agencies, and the maze becomes confounding.

If financial institutions are to be responsible to the needs of the market and to serve the public interest, I suggest that the regulatory channels and authority be clarified. The present bank regulatory structure is awkward enough without injecting scores of other players.

The climate of the Carter administration seems to be conducive to some simplification or modernization of the traditional bank regulatory agencies. That should be accompanied, in my opinion, by a clarification and simplification of the roles that other arms of government are to play in our institutional lives.

A second cause of regulatory delinquency, in my opinion, is that like new drugs, new regulations often have undesirable side effects which sometimes make the remedy worse than the malady.

Consider, for example, some of the rules propounded in the name of consumer protection. Ostensibly to protect consumers from unfair discrimination in the extension of credit, regulations now prohibit us from eliciting the kind of information we need to determine whether or not a loan applicant is worthy of credit. The net result of that kind of regulation will be: 1) a reduction in funds available to individual borrowers; or 2) an increase in the cost of such funds; or 3) more individual bankruptcies; or 4) all of these results, none of which serves the interests of the consumer, the depositor, or the stockholder.

Or consider the current disclosure fad. Appropriate and timely disclosure of facts pertinent to an investment decision is essential. But disclosure for disclosure's sake of detailed and often private material not only is irrelevant and confusing; it also produces some undesirable side effects. Many small and medium-sized companies feel foreclosed from the capital markets by the formidable and complex disclosure requirements of the SEC with the result that they turn to the commercial banks to fulfill capital needs—a function commercial banks should not need to perform. Furthermore, the disclosure fad risks disclosure of proprietary information, the deliberate exchange of which with a competitor would rankle an antitrust lawyer.

Sound marketing strategies for financial institutions require, it seems to me, an equally sound strategy by government. Government must declare its objectives, define its role, and pursue that role with some measure of predictability. Government strategy must recognize that the most important requirement of a banking system is public confidence. Without confidence of depositors and borrowers alike, no banking system can serve the economy. Proper ratio of capital to assets, proper classification of loans, proper accounting methods all are important only as they contribute to confidence.

Government should not judge its performance by the number of laws or regulations it imposes, nor by the number of agencies playing the regulatory game. The quality of government regulation can be measured only by the health of those regulated and the consequent quality and worth of their service to the public.

CONCLUSION

My whole effort has been to portray the influence of the economic environment on market planning in banking and to remind you of some of the fundamental premises that apply to banking under all economic conditions. Despite all efforts at planning, no one can predict the future with much certainty. I see around me banking institutions and banking services that neither I nor anyone could have conceived when I started in this business forty years ago.

Of one thing I am fairly certain, and that is that the process of change and adaptation to change will continue indefinitely, and financial institutions will continue to serve well and will continue to grow and to compete. Those institutions which will compete most effectively are those which are best able to understand their business environment and have the people and the resources to adapt imaginatively to the needs of that environment.

I would like to conclude with the same message that one of his teachers left with President Carter years ago: "We must adjust to changing times but never deviate from basic principles."

SEVEN

Marketing in a Goal-Oriented Organization:

The Texas Instruments Approach

J. Fred Bucy

President, Texas Instruments, Inc.

Marketing is but one leg of the "create," "make," and "market" functions of our business at Texas Instruments. Marketing strategy is a part of overall product strategy and product strategy is derived from corporate strategy. The "Marketing Concept" teaches that a company must focus on making what the customer wants rather than on selling what the company makes. This is sound advice, but it sometimes obscures major issues.

First, there is a belief by the stronger proponents of the "Marketing Concept" that competitive products are essentially alike and, therefore, success goes to the company that places the highest priority on marketing. This belief in the supremacy of marketing over the "create" and "make" functions is based on the idea that equal technology quickly becomes available to all participants in a market through the mobility of the technical community and today's communications. If this were true, competition for market share would be won or lost based on the mechanics of bringing the product to the user, as the concept suggests. But this simply is not the case in high-technology businesses. Marketing is vitally important, but technology is still a prime determinant.

ROLE OF TECHNOLOGY

Technology encompasses the thousands of detailed steps that are necessary to develop and manufacture a product. Science gives us knowledge but not concepts. Science may suggest what can be built, but only technology tells us how to build it. Frequently, technology alone permits us to invent new products to create markets, and new science is not always needed.

It's true that research findings often are made widely available—but the fruits of technology development rarely are. It is the lifeblood of competitive leadership and successful companies guard it jealously.

In the United States, government-sponsored research accounts for 53% of all research and development. Except for a few areas crucial to defense, these research findings are available to all. Yet certain companies consistently use this widely available research to produce superior products at lower prices, because they have developed their own superior technologies.

In addition to the free availability of government-sponsored research, private industry carries on active exchanges of research data, through technical symposia, the publication of papers, and the like. In fact, our dissemination of this information is so free that Eastern Bloc countries long have been amazed at the ease with which they can acquire what has been so costly for us to learn. But data acquired in the course of research do not reveal much of the "how to" needed to design and manufacture a product.

This know-how is so crucial that, at TI, we develop and build most of our critical manufacturing systems—and we would like to build all of them. First, this permits us to keep the performance characteristics of these systems confidential. Second, advances we make in design and manufacturing technology give us an important competitive edge. When production equipment is bought on the open market, by definition your productivity is about the same as that of your competition.

A company that enjoys life based on the assumption that there is no better way to design and produce a product than the currently available technology, can be in for a rude awakening. It has happened time and again in electronics, in business machines, and in calculators. Now it is happening in watches, with electronic watches displacing many mechanical watches, just as pin-lever movements displaced many Swiss movements a generation ago. Technology is by no means a constant in the competitive equation—to the contrary, it is a most important variable.

CORPORATE PHILOSOPHY AND GOALS

The second point that the "Marketing Concept" tends to obscure is that create, make, and market functions must be tightly interwoven in a system of management, corporate philosophy, and the corporate purpose. None of these functions can operate effectively by itself.

At TI, we define a basic corporate philosophy and enunciate corporate goals that represent good citizenship in the broadest sense. These goals establish the basic purpose of the corporation which neither we nor society should be allowed to forget. The basic purpose of corporations is to exercise wise stewardship in managing a large share of the physical assets of society. We strive to manage in a way that produces the maximum return to society—in new and better products, in creation and upgrading of jobs, in concern for the environment and in community well-being. In short, our purpose is to provide a higher living standard in both quality and quantity at lowest cost for employees, customers, and the community at large. Fulfilling this purpose requires that we make an adequate return on assets.

This basic philosophy is as old as TI. We formalized it in our Corporate Objective in 1961 and it has remained substantially unchanged. A fundamental element of this objective is a statement of corporate ethics—ethics that go further than just being within the law and that cover situations where no law exists. We communicate these standards to all employees and tolerate no deviation. Expedient compromises may promise short-term gains, but they can grow into a corporate cancer that will destroy the institution.

In addition to providing this ethical framework, our Corporate Objective defines the corporation's business intentions and goals: the kinds of business in which it will engage; the mix of business and geography; the company's posture toward employees, stockholders, customers, vendors, governments, and politicians; its specific profit goals and growth goals, and the methodology of growth—TI has always emphasized internal growth.

Within the Corporate Objective, we define a number of Business Objectives that specify the short- and long-range goals for major groupings of our business. These goals cover: the world-wide markets to be served, the products and services for these markets, and how to sell them; growth goals by product and market; technology requirements; and financial goals by product. This brings us to the company's Objectives, Strategies, and Tactics (OST) system.

OST provides an organization that overlays our decentralized product-customer center structure. It cuts across conventional organizational lines, so that an Objective manager often has Strategy managers reporting to him from various divisions of the company. A Strategy manager, in turn, may have Tactical Action Program (TAP) managers from many areas outside his conventional functional responsibility. As a result, a TI manager's responsibility usually exceeds his line authority. It also means that strategic organizations can quickly be formed or altered to meet rapid changes in our dynamic markets. Each Business Objective manager, Strategy manager, and TAP manager is responsible for achieving agreed-upon product goals.

FINANCIAL PLANNING

Basic financial models are established for all business areas, depicting both the operating statement and balance sheet indices. Based on the models, we develop complete financial plans for both operating numbers and balance sheet numbers, including as a minimum: a ten-year strategic plan; a three to five-year plan for facilities, manufacturing equipment, and technology; and a detailed plan for the next year for all organizational levels. A surrounding environment of computer-based management systems to handle the masses of data involved, in as near real time as possible, is required to keep these plans updated and effective—and in helping us measure ongoing business performance. Corporate management reviews are vital; board meetings are held monthly, and we hold quarterly operational reviews of each group.

ACHIEVEMENT OF PRODUCTIVITY GAINS

Plans to increase productivity encompass not only manufacturing but the entire organization. Special attention is given to overhead areas, where productivity gains are more difficult to achieve than they are in production. Our "People and Asset Effectiveness" programs formalize this corporate focus on productivity.

The heart of productivity improvement lies in programs of people motivation and involvement. We must help people understand the goals of productivity, profitability, and growth for the company and to see the direct relationship of these goals with their own career goals. An employee is a source of ideas and brains, not just a pair of hands. We strive to motivate employees to participate in planning their own work.

People must be recognized and rewarded for outstanding performance. They must share in the company's success. It is equally important to ensure that under-achievers are *not* rewarded—a process that is painful and often neglected. Growth opportunities for employees are created by policies of promoting from within, of posting new job openings, of establishing educational and training programs, and of stressing reward based on merit. To create real involvement, however, employees must be given a "piece of the action"— which means ownership in the company.

At TI a total compensation package called "Success Sharing" has been created for people who build a career in the company. It consists of wages and salaries that are competitive in our industry, a pension plan, a stock option purchase plan, and a profit-sharing plan paid in shares of company stock. The percentage of an employee's salary which he receives in profit-sharing each year is tied directly to worldwide profits, payroll, and assets.

Asset Management

The other dimension of our People and Asset Effectiveness concept is the intensive use of assets, including a deliberate policy of keeping plant and equipment at the cutting edge of productivity by an aggressive asset renewal cycle. Both asset renewal and corporate growth require careful allocation of capital, and these needs are encompassed by the financial models discussed earlier in relation to Business Objectives.

The models set the goals for asset use and return at a level that will generate enough cash through profits and depreciation to self-fund planned corporate growth without increasing the debt-to-equity ratio beyond a conservative level and without significant dilution of equity. We will not permit this emphasis on self-funding to limit growth, however, and we would willingly borrow rather than pass up major market opportunities.

But good asset management is essential. For a given profit level, it is asset turnover that fixes the level at which growth can be self-funded. In a period of capital shortages and high interest rates, the ability of a company to make new investments and to grow can be severely limited unless it can self-fund the bulk of its needs.

In summary, the most basic task of management is to find, keep, motivate, and promote the best people to achieve the corporation's purpose. Given the right people, the other basic elements of managing a corporation are to define its goals, to make certain they are measurable, and to establish a system for tracking the progress achieved and assuring necessary feedback. Corporate leaders must be teachers, for unless the goals can be convincingly communicated and unless the necessary corporate "culture" can be created to meet them, they will never be achieved. But they must be achieved if the corporation is to do its job in society.

An important measure of corporate performance is the ability to compete effectively in the marketplace.

Key Thrusts

Let's examine some of the concepts that are vital to winning this competition. The key thrusts may be summarized as follows:

Market Share
> Experience curves
> First in the market
> Shared experience
> Design-to-cost
> Price elasticity

Market Growth
> Growth/share matrix
> Capacity leads demand

Choice of priorities and allocation of resources

IMPORTANCE OF MARKET SHARES

The Experience Curve

To understand the value of market share and growth requires an understanding of experience-curve phenomena—a tool TI has used for more than twenty years.[1] Experience-curve history shows that each time the cumulative production of a product doubles, the cost to produce that product will decline by a fixed percentage. The experience curve for the worldwide production of integrated circuits is a classic demonstration of this predictable relationship as shown in Fig. 7.1. Products in most industries follow these regular price declines as a function of cumulative units, when the prices are measured in constant dollars. Even when measured in current dollars, as this curve does,

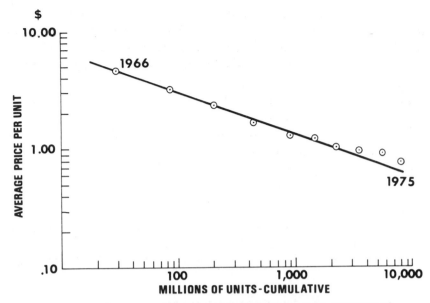

**Fig. 7.1 WORLD SHIPMENTS OF INTEGRATED CIRCUITS
LEARNING CURVE**

prices have withstood the higher inflation rates of recent years quite well.

Experience-curve behavior is especially striking in the solid-state electronics industry, because so many of the products are revolutionary and it is not unusual to see cumulative production double several times during the first few years.

The average consumer is well aware of this pricing behavior. Prices of transistor radios, for example, have declined from $49.95 to $2.50. Simple four-function handheld calculators have declined in price from $149.95 in 1972, to $6.00 or $7.00, and electronic digital watches have declined from several hundred dollars to less than $20.00. In all of these cases, as well as in our government, industrial, and computer businesses, it is the sharp expansion in production that presents the opportunity to reduce costs and improve productivity, making still lower prices possible.

The importance of market shares is illustrated in Fig. 7.2. The horizontal dashed line represents the current industry price. Companies A, B, and C have different cost positions depending upon the cumulative volume they have achieved as a result of different market shares. Company A has an excellent profit margin as the result of its large market share. Company B, on the other hand, is marginal, and Company C operates at a loss.

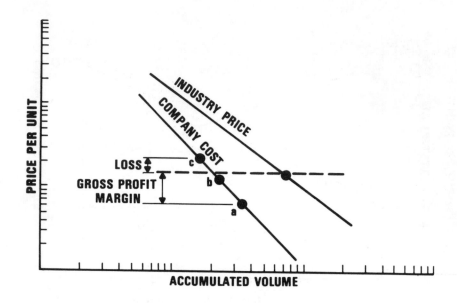

Fig. 7.2   VALUE OF MARKET SHARE

The axiom is that cumulative volume is paramount and, therefore, a company that participates in world markets has in inherent advantage over a company that confines itself to the production base of domestic markets only. Thus, the marketing function has a key responsibility in defining both the product characteristics and the system for distribution that will meet the requirements of world markets.

The Importance of Being First

A corollary to the value of market share is the importance of being the first to develop a new market. In Fig. 7.3 both companies have $1,000 start-up costs and a $90 unit cost in their first year of production. Both follow a 70% experience curve. A's unit price in Period One is $100, with a pretax profit of 10%.

A begins shipments in the First Period with 100 units, and increases them by 20% per period. B begins shipment in the Second Period with 100 units, but tries to play "catch-up" by increasing them at 30% per period.

The result is that A's cumulative pretax profit is a positive $948 at the end of the Second Period, and $6,972 at the end of the Ninth Period. But B does not achieve cumulative profitability until the end of the Ninth Period—and then, only $432.

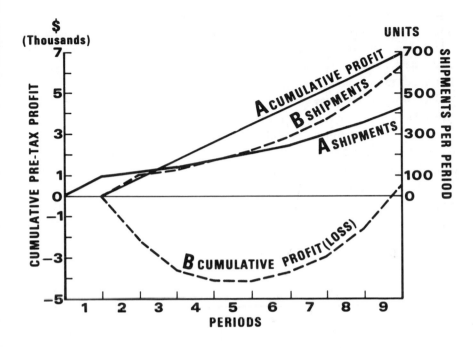

Fig. 7.3 THE VALUE OF BEING FIRST

The open secret of A's success is that its early entry into the market enables A to lead B down the experience curve, enjoying higher profit margins through the first seven periods.

Shared Experience

Cost advantage is gained not only from accumulated volume in the product produced, but also from accumulated volumes in related products. TI, with its semiconductor base, has this shared advantage in electronic products that have a high semiconductor content, for example, calculators, digital watches, minicomputers, and data terminals.

Design-to-Cost Approach

High volumes alone do not drive costs down. They merely provide the opportunity. At TI, *capitalizing* on this opportunity starts with "design-to-cost." This involves deciding today what the selling price and performance of a given product must be years in the future and designing the product and the equipment for producing it to meet both cost and performance goals. Stated another way, unit *cost* is a primary design parameter. It is a specification equal in importance to functional performance, quality, and service. This parameter takes the form of a timetable of steadily decreasing costs over the entire lifetime of the product.

The thrust of design-to-cost is to avoid designing into a product more performance than the market is willing to buy.

In part, the cost timetable is determined by the demand curve (or price elasticity curve), which shows the relationship of the price of a product to its potential sales volume. Unit price is the independent variable. Volume is the dependent variable. Typically these curves have a knee where the market growth rate in units increases rapidly once a certain price level is penetrated. Fig. 7.4 illustrates the relationship between volume and price.

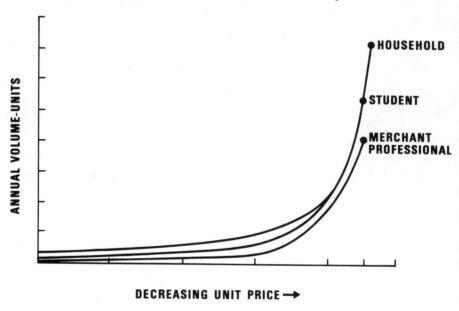

Fig. 7.4   RELATIONSHIP BETWEEN VOLUME AND PRICE

This kind of result is used to make the critical tradeoff between cost and performance that sets the final design parameters. Constructing this curve is one of the most challenging of all marketing problems. Perhaps the most effective approach, for both consumer and industrial products, is to segment the market carefully and then to conduct broad customer surveys within the segments the company expects to penetrate. The focal point of these surveys is what price the customer is willing to pay for specific product characteristics.

The cost timetable, in addition to being a function of the elasticity curve, is also a function of how quickly the knee of the curve will be approached, how large the start-up volume will be, and how quickly the volume increases on the experience curve.

The discipline created in an organization by setting pricing for the lifetime of a product is itself a powerful tool in the management of cost reduction. At the same time, the volume-dependent nature of the experience curve means that continual review and revision of cost goals are necessary as the future unfolds and volume requirements become more predictable. Thus, the design-to-cost approach becomes a forcing function for continuous productivity improvement throughout the entire lifetime of a product.

Distribute-to-Cost Approach

In addition to designing and manufacturing to cost, we must also distribute-to-cost. It's a mistake to devote thousands of engineering hours to wringing pennies out of manufacturing costs, only to have multitiered distribution add-back dollars to the ultimate price paid by the consumer. We feel a responsibility to be innovative in using the right distribution channels to make sure that manufacturing economies are passed through distribution to the customer. The experience-curve phenomenon that requires us to produce at continually lower costs, also requires that we distribute at continually lower costs.

For example, five years ago the small businessman who needed a mechanical four-function calculator had little choice but to call an office equipment dealer. Since a calculator then sold for perhaps $1000, the dealer could justify several personal sales calls, as well as personal service after the sale. His gross margin on the sale of this product would be $400 to $450 a unit.

Today, an electronic calculator selling for less than $100 will outperform that old $1000 machine. The margin available to the retailer who sells this product is about $35 per unit. This margin will not support the large sales and service organizations that previously existed. The result is that department stores now serve much of the small business market at substantially less cost to the customer. The high level of personal service is no longer required because of the higher reliability of the electronic calculator. Business equipment dealers have reoriented their thrust toward the high end of the programmable calculator market.

Since the founding of TI, we have worked to create an organization and an institutional "culture" in which continuing productivity increases, cost reduction, and the design-to-cost approach are viewed as moral obligations to society.

Price Policy

There are times when companies have no choice but to raise prices. But it is morally wrong for institutions to believe that just because their labor and material costs have gone up, they are automatically entitled to raise their prices on an equivalent basis. It is just as wrong to expect wages to go up automatically unless equal or greater gains can be made in productivity.

Price and wage increases will always be the first choice, though, unless design-to-cost and productivity improvement are thoroughly built into the company's behavioral pattern so that it actively, automatically, and continuously seeks to improve its mode of operation in order to give its customers more for less.

Applying design-to-cost principles enables us to price aggressively—a particularly important strategy in high-growth markets.

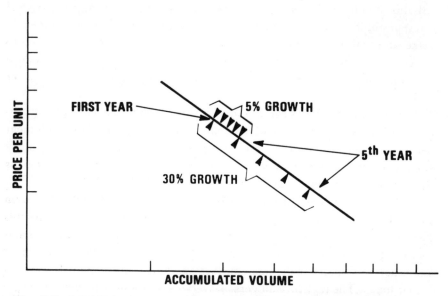

Fig. 7.5 DIFFERENT RATES OF MARKET GROWTH AND PRICES PER UNIT

Fig. 7.5 is an example which shows five years of travel down an experience curve. The widely spaced arrows show a 30% growth rate—a fast-growing market; those narrowly spaced, a 5% growth rate. With proper strategy, significant cost advantages and profitable positions can be gained very quickly in high-growth markets. Share can be gained without taking it directly from competitors and stimulating their counteractions.

MARKET GROWTH

Growth-Share Matrix Analysis

Both market segmentation and product innovation are important in planning the corporate business portfolio. The wristwatch is a good example. The market for traditional mechanical watches has had a low rate of growth. The leading producers made good profits. This changed suddenly when technological innovation made possible the digital watch, which has more capability and better accuracy at a lower price. The market size in units is now expanding at 100% per year and the leading producers have the opportunity of high-growth rate and high earnings. But those producers who didn't switch over fast enough have found themselves in no-growth, low-profit, poor-cash-flow situations.

Fig. 7.6 GROWTH-SHARE MATRIX AND ANALYSIS

We've stressed the importance of both market growth and market share in the competitive process. The *combined* impact is even more significant. The familiar growth-share matrix analysis technique developed by the Boston Consulting Group and TI is a useful analytical tool as shown in Fig. 7.6.

A business with low relative share in a low-growth market generally will have low earnings and poor cash flow. High-share, low-growth businesses will generate excess cash. In the high-growth, low-share quadrant, earnings will be low and cash flow negative. The combination of high share and high growth rate, properly optimized, yields good profitability and may or may not be self-financing, depending on the growth rate. The challenge is to maintain a balanced mix of products from each quadrant to balance cash flow.

The solid-state electronics industry is especially dependent on finding high-growth markets, because our processes inherently depend on high volumes to bring unit costs down. When manufactured in sufficiently high volumes, solid-state solutions are extremely cost effective.

Keep Capacity Growing Ahead of Demand

To maintain and gain market share in these fast-growing markets, capacity must keep ahead of demand. When prices decline steeply with accumulated volume, units grow faster than dollars as seen in Fig. 7.7. Net unit capacity must be added constantly just to hold market share. To achieve the cost reductions required, old equipment must be constantly replaced by new, more productive equipment. This suggests high capital expenditures for manufacturing equipment, short equipment life, a high probability that capacity will be

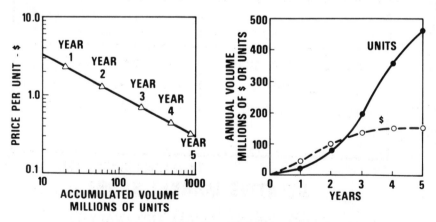

Fig. 7.7 KEEP CAPACITY GROWING AHEAD OF DEMAND

fully utilized, and fast depreciation. For example, TI's annual depreciation rate has been almost 15% of gross plant since 1964—a rate triple that of the companies making up the Dow-Jones Industrial's average.

DECISION PACKAGE RANKING

Keeping capacity ahead of demand—but not too far ahead—requires a strategic allocation of resources. This brings us to the final key thrust, the proper choice of priorities and the allocation of resources to implement strategies, a major function of TI's Objectives, Strategies, and Tactics system.

Decision Package Ranking is an integral part of the OST system. This technique permits us to compare requests for strategic resources made by the "create," "make," and "market" functions. Each *package* is so-called because it contains all the resources necessary to implement the strategy. Two of the vital criteria that decide the rank of a package are its potential contribution to market share and its position in a growth market.

Each level of organization ranks the packages within its responsibility; final ranking is accomplished by a corporate-level committee. Costs are accumulated from the top down to a cut-off point previously set as the discretionary funding level for the year. Programs below the line are placed in our "Creative Backlog" for consideration as funds become available.

Operating expenses are ranked separately, so that strategic expenses may be cross-ranked against them. In this way, we can trade-off strategies not only against each other, but against operating expenses as well.

Although we had been doing it for many years, we formalized Decision Package Ranking in 1968; it became known as Zero-based Budgeting in 1969.

It is largely through this process of allocating resources that we try to anticipate customers' needs and to create the products to meet those needs—generating new markets. These decisions, more than any other, determine the strategic directions of the company.

STRATEGIES FOR SUCCESS IN WORLD MARKETS

As we carry out these strategies, we remain acutely aware that all of the factors in the business equation are dynamic. Market share and market growth rates change continuously. New technology appears unpredictably. Competi-

tive responses can change the market picture overnight. We reevaluate resource allocation constantly and make many hard choices, because there are
never enough resources to do all the things we feel we should.

To summarize, none of these strategies can be successful without the
others, any more than marketing can be successful when treated as a separate
function of a business. Marketing and market strategy must permeate every
other function of the company. When overall strategic thinking becomes as
natural as breathing to every manager, we can expect to be successful in meeting the challenges and opportunities of the future.

Notes

1. Winifred B. Hirschmann, "Profit from the Learning Curve," *Harvard Business Review,* (January-February 1964,): pp. 125-39, and "Texas Instruments: All Systems
Go," *Duns Review,* (January 1967): p. 25.